Esther Macomber

MASTER WILL OF STRATFORD

THE MACMILLAN COMPANY
NEW YORK · BOSTON · CHICAGO · DALLAS
ATLANTA · SAN FRANCISCO

MACMILLAN & CO., LIMITED
LONDON · BOMBAY · CALCUTTA
MELBOURNE

THE MACMILLAN CO. OF CANADA, LTD.
TORONTO

MASTER WILL OF STRATFORD

A MIDWINTER NIGHT'S DREAM

IN THREE ACTS

WITH A PROLOGUE AND AN EPILOGUE

BY

LOUISE (AYRES) GARNETT

New York
THE MACMILLAN COMPANY
1916

CLAYTON F. SUMMY COMPANY,

64 East Van Buren St., Chicago.

The Compositions are as follows:

A WASSAIL-SONG	(Act I)
FAIRY-GO-ROUND (A Carousal)	Pucks' dance (Act I) Witch's dance (Act I) Fairies' dance (Act III)
A MAY-SONG	(Act II)
FOREST GAVOTTE	(Act III)
TITANIA'S LULLABY	(Act III)

MASTER WILL OF STRATFORD

CHARACTERS

WILL SHAKESPEARE, *nearly twelve years of age.*
MISTRESS JOHN SHAKESPEARE, *his mother.*
BETSY, *a neighbor, about twelve.*
THE WEE DICKUMS, *Betsy's brother.*
QUEEN ELIZABETH.
SIR THOMAS LUCY, *of Charlecote.*
A PEDLAR, *afterward* FILCH.
OBERON, *King of the Fairies.*
TITANIA, *Queen of the Fairies.*
THE LITTLE INDIAN BOY.
THE CONSTABLE.
ROBIN GOODFELLOW, *leader of the Pucks.*
COWSLIP
FIREFLY
WASP   } *Oberon's Pucks.*
PEPPER-CORN
CHALICE
CADENCE
DULCET   } *Titania's Fairies.*
MELODY
THE WITCH OF WIMBLE.
LADY-IN-WAITING *to Queen Elizabeth.*
FOUR MINSTRELS.
FRIAR TUCK, ROBIN HOOD *and other morris-dancers.*
Customers, bystanders and rustic singers.

(See Notes, *post*, for description of morris-dance.)

Scene: Stratford-on-Avon and neighborhood, 1575 A. D.

Prologue ⎫
Act I ⎭ The Shakespeare Kitchen.

Act II ⎫ The Forest of Arden   Day-time.
Act III ⎭   Night-time.

Epilogue,   The Kitchen.

The Prologue opens New Year's Eve, and the Epilogue New Year's morning. Acts I, II, and III, represent the dream during that interval.

PROLOGUE

SCENE: *The Kitchen in* JOHN SHAKESPEARE'S *house, Henley Street, Stratford-on-Avon, on New Year's Eve. In center rear, a door. At right of door, an oblong small-paned window, its sill, about three feet from the floor, bearing a prim row of potted plants. Right wall, center, a large open fireplace in which is a black pot over a low fire. A high-backed settle is at right and left of fireplace. A seat extends beneath the window from the settle at right rear corner of room. The seat of settle at right of fireplace raises. At right of door a clock stands; at left of door, a table. A basket of apples is on the table and above are shelves holding copper utensils. At rear left, a large churn. At center left, a door. At center front, a small table covered with an unbleached linen strip and bearing a bowl of milk, a spoon, a plate of bread and a dish containing small cakes. A lighted candle is on this table and another on the table at rear. At right front is a table prepared for ironing, with a basket near containing dampened clothes. The ironed garments are on the settle at left of fireplace. A medium sized basket hangs on the wall. A few chairs complete the furnishings.*

MISTRESS SHAKESPEARE *is ironing. She listens, puts down her iron and going to the door looks anxiously without. She closes the door. The clock strikes seven. She glances at the clock, then goes to the window. Seeing someone approach, she opens the*

3

door and admits BETSY *carrying her baby brother,*
DICKUMS.

MISTRESS SHAKESPEARE

Bless my heart, if it isna Betsy and the wee Dickums! Come you in, Betsy girl.

BETSY

[With a curtsy.]

Good den, missus.

MISTRESS SHAKESPEARE

What brings the two of you out tonight, child?
Dickums should have been tucked in this long while.

BETSY

It war lonesome enough sittin' in the dark to save
candles, wi' naught but the two on us—an' him asleep;
so I clapped a biggen on his head, and an old slop
'round him, an' here we be!

MISTRESS SHAKESPEARE

[Resuming her ironing.]

Are all your folk away?

BETSY

Ah-yea, missus. There be goin's-on at our cousin's
this New Year's Eve. Dickums is such a wee dilling,
an' me such a strappin' lass, I bide at home an' do the
motherin' o' him.

MISTRESS SHAKESPEARE

And a good little mother you are, with ever a babe in your arms or one tagging at your heels.

BETSY

I've had little brothers an' sisters to give drinks to by night an' wallops to by day, ever sin' I war knee-high to a stagger-bob.

MISTRESS SHAKESPEARE

You are a busy lass, Betsy.

BETSY

There be constant someone a-yelpin' for a tot o' milk or a shive o' summat, or bits an' bobs to do for mother. When I tell your Will, missus, how fore-wearied I get, he sez to me, "Betsy," sez he, "you shoodna forget to jog up your fancy. Fancy 'ud liven you prodigious," sez he.

MISTRESS SHAKESPEARE

[*Ceasing her ironing.*]

Yea—that is like my laddie. [*Resumes ironing.*] I canna tell what is keeping him so late. He should have been back by six o' the clock.

BETSY

Mayhap he went by Charlecote way. They do be a-sayin' the Queen is mekin' a day's visit to Sir Thomas and Lady Lucy. Her hankers arter a morsel o' quiet now an' then.

MISTRESS SHAKESPEARE

But Willie isna one for dalliance and making his mother longful for him. Sit you up by the fire, Betsy, and have an apple.

BETSY

I maut take a dab for Dickums.

[MISTRESS SHAKESPEARE *passes the basket of apples to* BETSY.]

MISTRESS SHAKESPEARE

Here are some scrumps and apple-johns, and one or two leather-coats and sourings. Help yourself right freely, lassie.

[BETSY *takes a couple of apples eagerly.*]

BETSY

An' I do be thinkin', missus, as how Dickums maut relish a pikelet.

MISTRESS SHAKESPEARE

Marry, to be sure. Have some cakes, and welcome.

BETSY

[*Eating heartily.*]

Dickums yent a scraily babe, full o' doctor's stuff. A dab or a dollop's all the same to Dickums. The wee lamb's a-sleepin' so I maut as well eat the apples an' pikelets mesel'—we shoodna be wasteful.

[*She puts him on the settle beside her. There is a knock.*]

MISTRESS SHAKESPEARE

Who comes knocking, I wonder? I hope it is no fell

news about my laddie. [*She opens the door and speaks in amazement.*] Sir Thomas Lucy! [*She curtsies with dignity.*] Your pardon, Sir Thomas, come you in.

SIR THOMAS

[*Entering.*]

Where is John Shakespeare?

MISTRESS SHAKESPEARE

He and some other o' the burgesses, sir, have gone to Coventry.

[*Sir Thomas taps the floor impatiently.*]

SIR THOMAS

Beshrew me! that is vexing.

MISTRESS SHAKESPEARE

Mayhap I can serve you, sir.

SIR THOMAS

Yea, you can—by keeping your slacken-twist of a son at home!

MISTRESS SHAKESPEARE

A slacken-twist? My laddie?

SIR THOMAS

Yea, your laddie—the one they call Will.

MISTRESS SHAKESPEARE

What harm do you seek to fasten on him, sir?

SIR THOMAS

He has been snaring pheasants in my park—caught in the act with a bird in his arms.

MISTRESS SHAKESPEARE

My boy has great love for creatures and gets together the maimed and ailing that he may nurse them till they be sound again.

SIR THOMAS

No doubt he snares that he may cure.

MISTRESS SHAKESPEARE

You have a bitter tone, Sir Thomas, and my lad is a good lad.

SIR THOMAS

Good lad, or bad lad, keep him away from Charlecote. I was passing your house and have troubled myself to give you warning. If your young giddypate so much as take a pace on my land, or look at one of my pheasants, he shall be punished soundly.

MISTRESS SHAKESPEARE

He were a poor spirited lad if he so much as went within breathing-space o' your grounds. My heart is built in the shape of a W. I believe in my Will.

SIR THOMAS

Believe, an it suit you, but mark what I say, and your bold bantling as well: if ever he cross my path to give me offense, be it tomorrow or a score of years hence, I shall deal him a double dose for good measure.

MISTRESS SHAKESPEARE

You are a liberal apothecary when it comes to double doses. Good e'en to you.

SIR THOMAS

Woman,—

MISTRESS SHAKESPEARE

Your pardon, sir, I have a rare fondness for the last word, and my tongue hangs like a clapper in the middle o' my mouth.

SIR THOMAS

I tell you—

MISTRESS SHAKESPEARE

Good e'en to you, sir. Can you find your way out? [*She holds open the door and Sir Thomas scowls as he goes toward it.*]

SIR THOMAS

I have this to say—

MISTRESS SHAKESPEARE

Be careful o' the step. That's right. [SIR THOMAS *disappears and she opens the door still wider*.] Whew! Condemn me for a chatterpie if I do not have to air the place of the man's spirit. There's fell need for the perfumer.

BETSY

[*Who has been all eyes for Sir Thomas and teeth for her dainties.*]

Yond be a brawlin', naggin' pickthanks, forever gettin' things all of a pother. [*Crooking her fingers.*] Wotna I like to set my ten commandments in his face? These apples and pikelets do be fine and toothsome, missus.

MISTRESS SHAKESPEARE

Help yourself, lassie.

BETSY

I maut be takin' a bittock, leastways a spot o' pikelet for Dickums.

MISTRESS SHAKESPEARE

What can be keeping my laddie?

[*A figure runs past the window and through the open door. It is the young Shakespeare. She throws her arms about him.*]

Will!

WILL

Yes, Mother, here am I, late o' the clock but early o' my desire.

[*He places his cloak, which he has carried bundle-wise, on the settle.*]

MISTRESS SHAKESPEARE

[*Closing the door.*]

What mean you, laddie?

WILL

My desire bade me stay till I could turn tailor and take fresh measure of a man and, having measured him, make new garments to fit him.

MISTRESS SHAKESPEARE

Ay, lad, I catch your meaning.

WILL

Good even, Betsy.

BETSY

Good den, Will.

WILL

The man whose measure I would take would find himself wearing, 'stead o' trunks large enough for Hercules, pinnies to fit Betsy's Dickums.

MISTRESS SHAKESPEARE

I ken the man.

WILL

Yes, Mother.

MISTRESS SHAKESPEARE

He was here and mortal inflamed against you, laddie.

WILL

Did he call me poacher?

MISTRESS SHAKESPEARE

Ay, that he did.

WILL

And you—what said you, Mother?

MISTRESS SHAKESPEARE

I said my lad wouldna poach and Willie, an I saw you do it with my own eyes, I wouldna believe it.

WILL

I must tell you what befell your scapegrace son.

MISTRESS SHAKESPEARE

Eat your bit of supper at the same time, laddie, and I'll finish some lated ironing. I canna rest till my work is done, even if it does make me iron of a New Year's Eve. And on the morrow I shall start the first day of the year in right proper fashion, by churning.

[*She has been getting ready to iron and Will has seated himself.*]

WILL

I meant to come straight home after I left Charlecote. I started by way of Tiddington Road and got as far as the bridge, but was so brimmed with heated thoughts I crossed the Meadows and went up by the Brake to Luddington.

MISTRESS SHAKESPEARE

And did the walk cool your hot thoughts?

WILL

Ay, when I came back as far as the footbridge by the

Mill and saw Trinity spire against the sky like an arch-angel's finger, I felt cool and soft in my thoughts and ready to come home to you.

MISTRESS SHAKESPEARE

The home nest's the place for bruised wings. But tell us o' the happenings at Charlecote.

WILL

I had heard it said the Queen and her ladies had come for a peaceful New Year's even, and had ridden forth for an airing. You know how I relished the sight of our Queen at Kenilworth last July, so I wandered up Charlecote way, hoping for a glimpse of her.

MISTRESS SHAKESPEARE

None could blame you for that.

BETSY

I war a-motherin' Dickums or I maut 'a gone.

WILL

Whilst I dallied, pretending the hedge was white with bloom instead of snow, a pheasant half hopped, half flew into the path before me, one wing broken and hanging pitifully.

MISTRESS SHAKESPEARE

The poor creature!

BETSY

They say pheasants do be mortal fine eatin'.

WILL

I reached for the bird to ease its sufferings; but, thinking I meant mischief, it led me a spanking chase. Before I was aware, we were in the Charlecote grounds and I had just seized the bird when the keeper clapped his hand on my shoulder.

BETSY

My faith! these be some doin's.

MISTRESS SHAKESPEARE

What did he to you, laddie?

WILL

He believed not a word of my story and hauled me, pheasant and all, to the high road. We had no more than gained it before who should come riding up but—

BETSY

The Queen! Lawk-a-dingin's, the Queen hersel'!

MISTRESS SHAKESPEARE

Sir Thomas Lucy!

WILL

Ay, both, and a small party of ladies and gentlemen. They drew rein and Sir Thomas inquired what the pother was about.

MISTRESS SHAKESPEARE

My poor lad!

WILL

He has but a handful of pheasants and sets such store by them he was stirred to a rage at the keeper's tale. The keeper thrust his hand into my doublet and drew out a cord. Then of a certainty they believed I had been snaring.

MISTRESS SHAKESPEARE

How came you by the cord?

WILL

I had it for top-spinning.

BETSY

Whut did they to you? An' whut did you to they?

WILL

When I saw they had writ poacher over me in tall letters I asked justice of the Queen.

BETSY

God mend me! Spoke ye to the Queen?

MISTRESS SHAKESPEARE

What said you, lad?

WILL

[*Laughing.*]

'Twas as good as the play.   I said: "Your Majesty, were I poacher and you near 'tis not pheasants I should pilfer."   "And why so, youngling?"   "Marry, I should try to poach a hare and not a pheasant." "Why a hare?" asked the Queen.   "I should try to poach a hair from your Majesty's golden fleece," quoth I.   "Oho, my March-chick, you are a Jason indeed!" she said, and fell to laughing.

MISTRESS SHAKESPEARE

My boy! how could you—to the Queen!

WILL

A queen at best is but flesh and blood, and wit may be royal wherever 'tis found.

BETSY

On, on, Will! whut more did ye?

WILL

Well, the upshot was she asked Sir Thomas to forgive this offense and let me have the bird to coax back to strength.

MISTRESS SHAKESPEARE

Said she those words: *forgive this offense?*

WILL

Oh, Mother, there's the rub!   She gave me my re-

lease yet believes me guilty. Were she the Queen I
held her she would have known I spoke true.

MISTRESS SHAKESPEARE

Ay, Willie.

BETSY

Whut 'came o' the bird?

WILL

'Tis here.

[*He goes to the settle and opens his cloak, displaying the pheasant.*]

MISTRESS SHAKESPEARE

Put the poor thing in this.

[*She hands him the basket from the wall. WILL puts the pheasant
in the basket and places it on the hearth.*]

BETSY

It war a fearsome adventure. It mun be grand to
go adventurin'. Things be mortal dull most whiles.

WILL

What have I told you, Betsy? Rouse your fancy
and adventures will hap as thick as bees around the
honey-pot.

BETSY

I caunt see whut use fancy be to a body.

WILL

It makes you see stories in men's eyes.

BETSY

That's brave to say, but whut 'ud a body's fancy do for a dilling like Dickums?

WILL

An you tire thinking on him as a babe, think on him as a man.

BETSY

A man! Dickums! That'd take more nor fancy— that'd take a prophet.

WILL

Not a prophet but a play-actor. Truly the least has his part to play. Dickums is a mewling babe in your arms, yet will he one day start for school, filling himself with Latin roots heavy for his digestion.

MISTRESS SHAKESPEARE

Then, ere you know, will he be courting the lasses and, though their locks be coarse and straight as old Roan's tail, making rhymed nonsense to their silken tresses.

WILL

Next will he be man, slaying and slashing with reckless blade.

MISTRESS SHAKESPEARE

Yea—and so will he act his part, on through middle age, and old age, and the old-old age that joins itself to babyhood.

WILL

That makes a circle o' life—a huge teething-ring on which men cut their wisdom. Ay, Betsy, your baby brother is become the hero of a tale.

BETSY

My wee lamb? Ho, lamb! ŏŏt like to be the hero of a tale?

WILL

Mock me not, Betsy. I shall be a weaver one o' these days and make whatsoever pattern I choose. I could make you into a merry shepherdess, or I could even make you into a princess,—an I would.

BETSY

Princess! *me!*

WILL

Ay, you. Mayhap I shall.

BETSY

I wotna care whut you made o' me, Will, so I be lass wi' time now an' then for play.

[*There is a rap on the window-pane. The face of a pedlar appears.*]

WILL

'Tis the pedlar I saw on Clopton Bridge,—dumb as a fish in speech and wits, poor fellow.

MISTRESS SHAKESPEARE

He canna talk, say you?   Bid him come in.

WILL

[*Opening the door.*]

Come you in and get a taste o' the fire.

[*The pedlar enters with his tray of trifles and goes to the hearth. He is brute-like in his stolidity.*]

MISTRESS SHAKESPEARE

Sit you down, good man.   [*He shakes his head.*] Well, if you canna, let us see if you've aught we would buy.   [*She and* WILL *look at the tray.*]   I'd like to get a bit o' something for your father, laddie.

WILL

There seems naught for men but masks, and father's face is too good to cover.

MISTRESS SHAKESPEARE

I'll get him a kerchief.   That's rare enough to be a treat.   How much, Pedlar?

[*He makes signs with his fingers.*]

WILL

Here is a string o' blue beads—a young maid's rosary.   Put it 'round your neck, Betsy.   [*To his mother.*]   I'll buy it out of the New Year's coin father gave me.

[PEDLAR *again tells the price by signs.*]

BETSY

For me? O Will! Thanky! I be mortal glad you dinna get me needles, or aught that's useful. An' I be glad too, I 'aven't a Adam's apple, or it wotna fit. Doant I look brave?

MISTRESS SHAKESPEARE

That you do. I'll get the money for you, Pedlar.

[*Exit* MISTRESS SHAKESPEARE *door, left.* WILL *goes toward rear to count out the pedlar's pay.* BETSY *is engaged with her new treasure. The pedlar empties the remainder of the apples and cakes into a bag at his side. Enter* MISTRESS SHAKESPEARE.]

MISTRESS SHAKESPEARE

[*As she and* WILL *pay the pedlar.*]

Eat some cakes afore you go out into the night. [*Sees the empty dish.*] What's happed to the cakes? They were in the dish but a moment since! There may be more.

[*Goes to table at rear.* WILL *stirs the fire. The pedlar, fearing detection, empties the cakes back into the dish.* WILL *turns.*]

WILL

Mother, the cakes have leaped into the dish. They must be full o' yeast to rise and fall so lightly. [*Smiling.*] Help yourself, Pedlar. As to apples, I'd offer you some but more might give you a touch o' the colic.

[PEDLAR *goes to the door.*]

MISTRESS SHAKESPEARE

Come you again, Master Pedlar.

[*He nods sullenly. Exit* PEDLAR.]

BETSY

There be a man you couldna find any stories in. He be cold an' muddy as a eel.

WILL

O Betsy! will you never see? I could light his eyes, loose his tongue—yea, wake him from the dead. 'Tis the miracle that tugs at me night and day.

BETSY

I'd see if I could, Will. Anyways I know beads when I see 'em. We mun go now. Dickums relished the pikelets an' apples right well, an' me too, missus.

MISTRESS SHAKESPEARE

Wrap you up, lassie.

BETSY

My beads'll keep me warm.

WILL

I'll see you home.

BETSY

Nay, Will. I be goin' to stop at the Pringles 'round the corner. God buy ye.

MISTRESS SHAKESPEARE

Come again, Betsy girl, you and your Dickums.

[*Exeunt* BETSY *and* DICKUMS. MISTRESS SHAKESPEARE *and* WILL *put away the ironing and carry the two tables from the front to the rear, left.*]

WILL

Mother, instead of going a-merry-making tonight with the lads, I would ask something else of you.

MISTRESS SHAKESPEARE

Speak out, laddie. When have I found it in my heart to deny you aught I could grant?

WILL

Let me for this night stay up as long as I would.

MISTRESS SHAKESPEARE

And not go out with the lads on New Year's Eve? Marry come up! 'tis a right droll wish.

WILL

You know my Christmas book that Sir Thomas gave me at Grammar School.

MISTRESS SHAKESPEARE

Thomas Hunt, God speed him!—not Thomas Lucy.

WILL

Methinks Hunt is short for goodness and Lucy

short for Lucifer. Besides, Thomas Hunt doth spell
Thomas with one S and Thomas Lucy perforce must
use two!

MISTRESS SHAKESPEARE

Fie, lad! see that your wrongs make not your tongue
over sharp. But what o' the book your master gave
you?

WILL

I would sit up this night, burn as many candles as I
choose, and read to my soul's contentment.

MISTRESS SHAKESPEARE

I see no reason why you shouldna. Your father is
away, Gilbert and Joan are at our cousin's till the
morrow, and the wee Anna and Richard sound asleep
this long while. Stay you up, an you wish. Help me
with the churn, laddie. [*They bring it forward and
place it at center, left.*] Now is it ready for the morrow.
'Tis fine sport coaxing cream to change itself to butter.

WILL

[*Peeping inside the churn.*]

'Twould be a bonnie hiding place for merry-minded
goblins! Oh, Mother, I shall have a brave evening with
the fairies. Ovid has made me friends with Titania,
and the book I would read is full o' the doings o' the
magic people. There is a king called Oberon and
tonight all of us will gallop away on a slant o' silvery
moonshine.

MISTRESS SHAKESPEARE

Bless you, my lad. Would I could join you in your fairy caperings.

WILL

See the kettle! 'Tis a cauldron to breed witches and their tailless kind.

MISTRESS SHAKESPEARE

Your mind is a busy cauldron but it breeds more than witches.

WILL

[*Going to the window.*]

We shall have a moon tonight. There is something about moonlight that searches out every nook and corner of me and drenches me with music. Some day—oh, Mother, I have a desire so tall that it tucks its head into the very lap of heaven.

MISTRESS SHAKESPEARE

I know it, laddie. You are all a-shimmer with lovely fancies. God shield you, my dearest.

[*She kisses* WILL *and leaves through door, left.* WILL *takes the book out of his doublet and with a sigh of joyousness throws himself before the fire, a candle near his open page.*]

END OF PROLOGUE

ACT I

The curtain reascends immediately on a darkened stage.
RUSTICS *are heard singing in the distance, their*
song growing clearer as they pass the Shakespeare
home, and again becoming fainter as they move on.
A half-moon rises and shines through the window.

RUSTICS

[*Singing.*]

Here we come on New Year's Day
A-singing, a-singing,
Hearts and songs and steeple-bells
A-ringing, a-ringing.
Come ye out and fill ye up,
Take a whiff and drink a sup—
'Tis the steaming wassail cup
We're bringing, we're bringing.

We would give to each of you
A warning, a warning:
Let no spirit go today
Forlorning, forlorning.
Thank your God for what you've got,
Thank your God for what you've not,
Thank Him for the wassail pot
On New Year's in the morning.

[*The clock strikes twelve. The chimes of Stratford ring out.*
Tiny lights flash, coming from FIREFLY *hiding near the fire-*

place, Cowslip *under the table,* Wasp *behind the churn, and* Pepper-Corn *in the shadow of a chair. The lid of the settle is raised and a fifth light appears.*]

ROBIN

[*Within the settle.*]

Whist!

[*In a twinkling he and his* Pucks *fly out of hiding.* Robin, *standing in the path of the moon's rays, holds aloft his spark of light.*]

Shine, ye servitors of light!
Drive away the bat of night.

[*The gloom lifts and they join hands and caper in a dance, with leap-frog pranks and elfin riot.*]

ROBIN

Attention, sprites!

[*The* Pucks *line up.*]

PUCKS

Ready!

ROBIN

There is heavy business on foot.

PUCKS

[*Hopping, each with hand on foot.*]

Ouch!

ROBIN

What ails you?

COWSLIP

Please, Robin, as you said there is heavy business on foot, my toes did hurt as if a cask had rolled upon them.

WASP

My toes ache not, but my instep feels as 'twere on fire.

FIREFLY

'Tis not my toes nor my instep, oh Robin-come-bobbin', 'tis my heel. I vow 'tis rosy with pain.

PEPPER-CORN

You are lucky 'tis but your instep, toe and heel. I have a monstrous prickling from ankle to thigh bone.

My toes!   ⎫
My instep!   ⎬ PUCKS [*in rapid*
My heel!   ⎪   *succession.*]
My ankle and thigh bone! ⎭

ROBIN

[*Disdainfully.*]

An you had your deserts your merrybones would be snapped like *that!* Let me know when you are ready to hearken to reason.

PUCKS

[*Lining up sedately.*]

We are ready.

ROBIN

I am come on a quest for Oberon. Our King and Queen have had a monstrous falling out.

COWSLIP

Already have the winds blown the rumor to our ears.

[*The* PUCKS *shake their heads gravely.*]

WASP

Has it not to do with a babe?

FIREFLY

A little Indian boy?

ROBIN

Yea; the son of Titania's friend who dwelt in the land of lotus blossoms and savory sandalwood. When she, being mortal, died, Titania brought home the babe.

PEPPER-CORN

'Tis said he is bronze of color.

COWSLIP

And that our Queen dotes on him.

ROBIN

Oberon wishes the changeling for his own—to be reared as his henchman. The Queen refuses to yield him the child, which doth set the King at loggerheads with her.

PEPPER-CORN

Marry come up! 'tis a pretty pother.

FIREFLY

What have you to do with their tempest, Robin?

ROBIN

I am to get the babe and give him into Oberon's keeping.

PUCKS

How?

ROBIN

The Witch of Wimble is to place him in my hands.

WASP

The Witch of Wimble is a brewer of mischief.

COWSLIP

And likes to stick her long gaunt finger into other people's pies.

PEPPER-CORN

She drives a hard bargain.

FIREFLY

How came she to do aught for you?

ROBIN

Beshrew me, if I be not a wondrous sharp fellow!

I am to give the Wimble Witch a paring from the Duchess of Bannister's finger nail in exchange for the Indian boy. 'Tis the hour for the signal.

[*He goes to the fireplace and raps on the pot three times.*]

> Wimble Witch,
> Swim the ditch!
> Wade the mire!
> Brave the fire!
> Break the bars!
> Leap the stars!
> Which and whither,
> Blood and blither,
> What I wait for
> Bring me hither!

[*There is a puff of red smoke and the* WIMBLE WITCH *emerges, a baby hanging over her shoulder. She wears a scraggly beard and has a long right forefinger.*]

WITCH

Hoot! hoot! thou owl of night.

[*Sound of winds.*]

Dim the moon in thy flight.

[*The light lowers.*]

Bah! I like not such giddy brightness. Well, well, Robin Goodfellow! have you brought me the paring?

ROBIN

Ay, Goody.

WITCH

Give it hither.

ROBIN

Give me first the babe.

WITCH

Not till I lay hands on your paring.

ROBIN

I must have the babe before I give it you.

WITCH

Two rogues drive a slow bargain.

ROBIN

Speak for yourself, an you will, but I am no rogue.
My name belies it—Goodfellow.

WITCH

Ay, but what o' your name *Robin?* Is not he that's
robbin' a robber?

COWSLIP

Give me the babe, Goody, and, Robin, give you the
paring to Firefly. When I say the word, we shall see
that each gets his own.

ROBIN

Are you of a mind to it?

WITCH

Yea, 'twere best.

[*She tosses the baby to* COWSLIP *and* ROBIN *gives the paring to*
FIREFLY.]

COWSLIP

Humblety, bumblety, huggermaree,
Tickety, clockety, one, two, three.

[ROBIN *joyously receives the baby, handling it awkwardly, and
the* WITCH *clutches the paring.*]

WITCH

At last! Now will the upstart Duchess do my
bidding.

ROBIN

What's to do with 'em?

WITCH

With what?

ROBIN

Babes.

PUCKS

Yea, what's to do with 'em?

WITCH

Milk! Milk! Milk! Plenty o' milk! Fill 'em full o'
milk. But mind your own brat. I have my precious
paring.

[*The* WITCH *dances, then disappears within the fireplace.*]

ROBIN

Good riddance! Let us see our noses; this witch-
light pleases not my fancy.

Shine, ye servitors of light!
Drive away the bat of night.

[*The room lightens. The baby cries.*]

Deuce take it! 'tis a nuisance.

FIREFLY

Milk! plenty o' milk!

WASP

The Wimble Witch said so!

PEPPER-CORN

Ay, but where's it to be found?

COWSLIP

The churn!

ROBIN

Marry, you are right. [*He tosses the crying baby into the churn, upright. There is a lusty yell.*] Verily, 'tis a milk-curdling sound! [*Another cry, then silence.*] Yea, drink your fill, inchling! Lap up the cream with your little pink tongue. Who says it is difficult to care for babes? Mayhap bronze-face will now turn whey-face.

COWSLIP

Hist! a step.

[*They disappear within their former retreats. There is a knock. Enter* WILL, *left, dressed as in the Prologue. He goes to door, rear, and opens it. The threshold is empty for a moment until* BETSY, *in the costume of a picture-book shepherdess, jumps out of hiding.*]

BETSY

[Suddenly, as she comes into view.]

Boo!

[She enters smiling.]

WILL

'Tis plain to see, Betsy, you are not too timid to say Boo! to a goose.

BETSY

It is not geese I fear—'tis *wolves*. But my flock is safe sheltered, even to the blackest sheep o' them all.

WILL

Had I your crook, faith, I'd use it to drive into the fold the solemn-souled folk o' Stratford.

BETSY

They who count it a sin to smile—like Sullen Jim, the tinker.

WILL

Ay, his face is so long his chin is red and calloused where he hath tripped on it. But smile or scowl, 'tis a work-a-day world and I must try my hand at churning—yet who would say that changing rivers o' cream into mountains o' butter be not magic? *[He tries to work the dasher.]* What ails it?

BETSY

Here! get you aside. 'Tis a maid's work, not a man's.

[The dasher will not work, and try as she will, BETSY cannot churn.]

A plague on the thing! 'Tis bootless churning.
[*There is a loud wail.*] It seems to come from *here*.

[*Points in alarm at the churn.*]

WILL

I'll look within.

BETSY

Are you not fearful?

WILL

'Tis a maid's part to churn; a man's not to be afraid.

[*Goes to the churn and pulls out the baby.*]

BETSY

A babe!

WILL

Faith, a very milksop!

[ROBIN *and the* PUCKS *leap out and circle around the children.*]

WILL

[*Good humoredly.*]

You are bedlam let loose! Cease your hubbub and
tell us who you are.

Robin Goodfellow. ⎫
Cowslip. ⎪
Firefly. ⎬ ROBIN and the PUCKS [*in rapid*
Wasp. ⎪ *succession, bowing.*]
Pepper-corn. ⎭

WILL

Well met, good people. [ROBIN *stands on his head.*]
You silly goblin—standing on your north when you
should be walking on your south! Pray tell us how a
babe and butter got so strangely mixed.

ROBIN

[*Scrambling to his feet and seizing the baby.*]

He is my charge.

BETSY

For shame! handling him like a meal sack. You are
as clumsy as if you came from Bergamo. [*She stamps
her foot.*]   Give him to me, you saucy manikin. [*She
takes the baby and cuddles him.*]   My poor lamb! my
wee nestling!

WILL

How came you by the babe?

ROBIN

I am its guardian. The Wimble Witch seized him
from Titania and placed him in my hands. I am to
give him into the keeping of Oberon who fancies him
for his own.

BETSY

Is not Titania his mother?

ROBIN

His foster-mother.

BETSY

Then why does she yield him, even to Oberon, her lord?

ROBIN

Pouf! She has naught to say about it. The Witch and I saw to that.

[*The* PUCKS *play leap-frog and cut up antics.*]

WILL

[*Aside to* BETSY.]

That wight has stolen the babe.

BETSY

Poor Titania!

WILL

Let us restore the boy to her.

BETSY

A right sound thought. We'll do it. But how get away?

WILL

Send Robin and his crew on an errand. Ho, Robin! ho, Pucks!

ROBIN and the PUCKS

Ay, ay, sir.

WILL

How do you expect this babe to drink milk and get

his rightful nourishment unless he take it from a bottle?

ROBIN

[*Scratching his head.*]

Do babes take milk out o' bottles?

BETSY

Of course, addlepate.

WILL

A fine guardian you, to give milk to your babe by throwing him into a churn!

ROBIN

It has a foolish sound. Marry, sir, what mortal fools we fairies be!

WILL

Hie you hence and bring back a nursing bottle, and let not Time, the old nag, go limping with you. Ride him hard and dig in the spurs.

ROBIN

Up, boys, away! But where, good sir, may the magic bottles be found?

WILL

At the apothecary's, slim-wit!

COWSLIP

His shop is but two hoots and a hurdle from the Golden Lion.

ROBIN

Forward.

[*Exeunt* Pucks.]

WILL

Now must we ride Time harder than I did counsel Robin.

BETSY

Whither?

WILL

West to Sanctus, thence south to the Brake.

BETSY

Ay, a Fairy Queen should not be far from the Brake.

WILL

Should I not have a staff, or wherewithal to protect you and the babe?

BETSY

That you should, Will.

WILL

I would I had a sword. I know!—the huge knife with which mother cuts the loaf.

[*Runs to table and gives a cry.*]

BETSY

What is it, Will?

WILL

Behold the changeling! The bread knife has turned sword. [*He displays the sword, then proudly claps it to his side. He feels his chin.*] Had I but a beard! But come! lean seconds make fat minutes.

[*Exeunt* WILL, BETSY *and the* INDIAN BOY, *leaving the door open. There is a puff of red smoke in the fireplace and the* WITCH *comes forth.*]

WITCH

West to Sanctus, thence south to the Brake. Ha! 'tis time the Wimble Witch stirred puddings with her finger. [*Stirs with her forefinger.*] I'll have my way in this or may I lose my bonnie beard. [*Rush of winds.*] Ay, there be forces still at work for the Witch of Wimble.

[*Exit* WITCH *through fireplace.*]

FILCH

[*The* PEDLAR, *off stage.*]

Come buy of Filch,
Come buy of Filch,
Come buy of Filch, the Pedlar.

[*He appears in the open doorway, the dumb and stolid pedlar of the Prologue awakened to a rollicking alertness. A large, open sack is strapped to his shoulder. He looks around the room with a merry glance, goes to the table, left, slyly takes up a candlestick, starts to put it into his sack, then with a shrug replaces it on the table. He goes off calling lustily.*]

Come buy of Filch,
Come buy of Filch,

Come buy of Filch, the Pedlar.
He'll drain your cup,
And snap you up,
And prove a merry meddler.

[*There is a far-off tinkling of bells. It grows nearer.* TITANIA
and her train enter eagerly and peer in and out of corners.]

TITANIA

O Chalice! Cadence! Dulcet! Melody! He is not
here—of a truth he is not here!

CHALICE

Are you sure the Bullfinch sent you hither?

TITANIA

Yea, Chalice, he said here, in this very room. And
not alone the Bullfinch saw Robin with the babe, but
the Hornéd Owl who lives in the Brake. They peeped
through the window.

MELODY

May Melody turn Discord if Robin be not made to
smart for crossing you.

CADENCE

And such a darling babe, with his pretty bronze
skin and his big brown eyes!

TITANIA

I think—yea, I am certain—my heart is breaking.

FAIRIES

Heart!

TITANIA

Said I heart?   Well, verily, by the threefold Diana,
I believe I am growing one.

CHALICE

Why think you that?

TITANIA

[*Folding her hands over her heart.*]

I have a sad feeling here.

MELODY

'Tis a sorry business.

TITANIA

[*Reaching out her hands on both sides.*]

And as if the world were a vastly bigger place than
it is, and I were lost in it.

DULCET

I've never felt like that—have you, Cadence?

CADENCE

Nay, I have never felt sad or lost.

TITANIA

O, Dulcet, mine eyes!

DULCET

Your eyes, sweet mistress?

TITANIA

Something like dew escapeth them.

DULCET

[*Drying them with a bit of her frock.*]

I've not seen the like before.

CHALICE

You forget. When the little gooseherd was for-saken by her lover, do you not remember how dew ran down her cheeks?

DULCET

And sparkled in the moonlight?

TITANIA

I remember. 'Twas said those were tears.

CADENCE

Then that dew—oh, that dew from your eyes is—

TITANIA

Tears. These must be *tears.* Now do I know I am growing a heart.

MELODY

What can a fairy do with a heart?

TITANIA

'Twould be monstrous useful with a babe.

[*Enter* ROBIN *and his fellows lugging a large stone jug.*]

ROBIN

Here is the nursing bottle. Filch, the Pedlar, from whom I bought it, says 'tis the only one in town.

TITANIA

Robin!

[ROBIN *and the* PUCKS *bow and scrape.*]

ROBIN

Celestial Titania—

TITANIA

Where is my babe?

ROBIN

Is he not here?   Then that's what I would know,— where is he?

TITANIA

Know you not, of a truth?

ROBIN

Nay, he was here when I started for the bottle. Do I speak true?

PUCKS

He speaks true.

ROBIN

Mayhap he is in the churn. [*Looks within.*] Butter!
'Tis full of butter! The babe hath churned it by his
frisky gambolings.

TITANIA

What shall we do? O Robin! I could find it in this
new heart to forgive you, would you do your best to
find him. I would rather Oberon had him than he
should be lost.

ROBIN

'Tis a big world.

CADENCE

For a new babe.

CHALICE

Ay, to be lost in.

ROBIN

We will seek him high and low—will we not, lads?

PUCKS

Ay, ay, sir!

TITANIA

And we will search the green earth till we wear it
brown with our footfalls ere we forsake our quest—
is it not so, Fairies?

FAIRIES

As true as true.

ROBIN

Which way shall we go?

TITANIA

I have a fancy to seek him in the Brake. Let us first to the south, then west to the Brake.

WITCH

[*Appearing in a puff of red smoke from the fireplace.*]

Nay, you are wrong. I would do you a service. The lad, Will, and the wench have taken the babe and plan to sell him to a childless prince.

TITANIA

Tailless rat! How dare I believe you?

WITCH

By my bonnie beard, I speak true.

TITANIA

Then which way went they?

WITCH

I heard them say, "First east, then north."

TITANIA

My thanks, dame. Fairies, hence!

ROBIN

Forward, lads!

TITANIA

[*As her Fairies and the* PUCKS *stream out into the night.*]

Haste! ye eager, twinkling feet.
Be ye valiant, be ye fleet;
Be ye harbingers of joy;
Bring ye tokens of my boy.

[*Exit* TITANIA.]

WITCH

Hoot! hoot! thou owl of night.

[*Sound of winds.*]

Dim the moon in thy flight.

[*The light lessens.*]

Ay, silly-pates, look your fill.   Who says this finger
has not the gift of stirring other people's puddings?
Stir and linger, stir and linger,
Poke and pry, thou busy finger.

[*The cock crows.   The* WITCH *rushes to the fireplace.   There is a
puff of red smoke and she disappears.   The cock crows again.*]

ACT II

SCENE: *A clearing in the Forest of Arden. It is the afternoon of May-day. A grassy knoll is near the right front. Trees and bushes circle the clearing. Country folk move back and forth, bubbling with pleasure in the day and scene.*

FILCH *has a tray suspended from his neck on which are masks, trinkets, ballads rolled and tied with ribbons, and an open sack, as in Act I. From time to time he deftly removes a purse or trifle from one of the crowd. He is industriously hawking his wares.*

FILCH

Come ye one and come ye many,
Bits and bobs for half a penny,
And if you would spend a shilling
Take my trayful, an you're willing.
Fortunes by the hour I'll tell you,
Ballads by the yard I'll sell you.
Any tidbit you are wishing
Name, that I may do the dishing.
Come you sweet, and pay so little
'Twill be but a fairy's tittle.
Come you sour and full o' trouble
Filch will joy to charge you double.

LASS

Please, Master Filch, read my fortune.

FILCH

Your fortune is plain in your face—and yet, God wot, 'tis not a plain face.

LASS

What read ye there?

FILCH

A marvel of nature: that cherries and tulips are one and the same, and being plucked should bring a high market price.

[*There is a laugh and the lass is discomfited.*]

LASS

You'll get na pay for that!

FILCH

I had hopes that in payment you would shake down just one cherry for me.

[*The crowd guffaws. A second lass puts forth her hand.*]

SECOND LASS

Prithee, look at that, Master Pedlar.

FILCH

A smooth dial; a white dial.   You would know what o'clock by it?   It says your sun is well up in the heavens and has cast no shadows for you.

SECOND LASS

But, good Master Pedlar, donna you see any—lads?

FILCH

Lads? Nay.

SECOND LASS

[*Pouting.*]

I donna believe you.

FILCH

Lads, nay, but *lad*—yea! There is one lad so much at home he has driven off all t'others. He looks as if he were come to stay.

BUMPKIN

[*Elbowing up and taking the lass by the arm.*]

May I eat naught but dunch-dumplings, Pedlar, if 'tisna true. Gi' me a smudge, lass, an' say the word.

[*She runs into the crowd, he pursuing.*]

FILCH

[*Holding up a small bottle.*]

Here be May-day dew that I bottled at dawn. 'Twill make the complexion as clear as the bells o' Trinity steeple. Only a few bottles left. [*Aside, with a wink.*] Dipped fresh from the Avon, within the hour!

[*A bumpkin enters on a run, chased by two or three laughing lasses. He wears a devil's mask, with horns, and ducks in and out of the crowd until captured. They lead him forward.*]

ONE OF THE LASSES

Master Pedlar, the Old Harry's horns be horns o'

plenty and he wishes to pour some o' your baubles on us.

FILCH

Good devil! Generous devil! They will make o' you afore long a smug, respectable devil. [*The girls busily select their gewgaws from* FILCH'S *tray.*] Here be straws, oaten straws—the very straws themselves— with which Cupid—the sly-boots!—tickled the chin of his lady love. Come, worthies, and buy. [*Aside.*] Fresh from Farmer Goodman's haystack!

YOUTH

Whut good be they to a body?

FILCH

What good, ye ask? Why, just as Cupid tickled the chin of his wench and caused her to snigger, so may ye try it on the chin o' your lass and make her to smile on you. Na smile, na pay.

YOUTH

That do be worth tryin'. Gi' me a mortal fine one.

FILCH

Here 'tis—a tawny, oaten straw, Cupid's own.

[YOUTH *takes it and tickles the chin of a lass. She giggles riotously. The youth claps his knee with delight and pays* FILCH. *Enter* WILL *and* BETSY, *the latter carrying the* INDIAN BOY.]

BETSY

[*To Will.*]

Mayhap someone here can tell us.

WILL

[*To a by stander.*]

Good morrow, sir. Can you tell us where dwells
Titania, the Queen?

BYSTANDER

Queen o' whut?

WILL

The Fairies.

BYSTANDER

Na, I ken naught o' the Queen o' the Fairies.

FILCH

[*Scenting customers.*]

Young sir, I see by your sword and babe you are
both a man of action and a man of family.

WILL

I am neither, wag, as you know.

FILCH

You have me hipped. Command me.

WILL

We seek a Queen called Titania. Know you where
she may be found?

FILCH

Alack, young sir, your Queen I know not. But have

you heard that our good Queen Bess is to witness the morris-dancers and the May-pole?

BETSY

The Queen, Will? Shall we see the Queen?

WILL

Yea, we shall stay. Perchance she may aid us.

BETSY

Ho, little lamb! You shall see our Queen with your very own peepers.

[FILCH *has removed* WILL'S *purse which hung at his side. The baby cries and* FILCH *is all genial solicitude. He shakes a dried gourd enticingly.*]

FILCH

Lookee, you lusty recklin. Listen to the music. [*The cries cease.*] He has a marvelous ear for music, good sir. You should buy this for him.

WILL

Faith, I'll do it. [*Misses his pouch.*] Soul and body o' me! My purse has been taken.

BETSY

Surely, you mistake.

WILL

Certes, 'tis gone. And my new mill-sixpence that I did hold for a wishing-piece!

FILCH

Alackaday! What scape-gallows could ha' done this fell thing?

WILL

Now I cannot buy the babe his bauble.

FILCH

'Tis top-full sorry business. Filch would ever do a good turn an he could. Make for me a ballad or couplet or what-not, in payment for this monstrous fine charmer, and you shall keep it for your bronzy brat.

WILL

Agreed, Master Pedlar. I'll whip up my muse.

> Filch thou art and Filch thou'lt be,
> Too much Filch by half for me.
> Filch by name and Filch by trade,
> Filch, thy fortune's good as made,
> For thou'lt mount to higher things—
> E'en to Tyburn spread thy wings.
> Whilst in comfort swinging there
> Thou canst steal a breath of air.

[*There is a round of laughter in which* FILCH *is foremost.*]

FILCH

Take the gourd, boy. May all my teeth be strung on lute strings and hung in the Old Harry's barber

shop, if you have not earned it! Marry, what have
we here? [*Stoops.*] Your purse!

[*Hands it to* WILL.

*Lutes and singing are heard. A lad runs in breathlessly from the
right.*]

LAD

Make way! Make way! Our Queen be a-comin'!
Our Queen be a-comin'!

[*A wave of eagerness stirs the crowd, and it falls back, though in-
clining expectantly toward the approaching company. The
strumming and singing have grown louder and the* MIN-
STRELS *stroll in, followed by* QUEEN ELIZABETH (*whose
costume is topped by a crown*), *a* LADY-IN-WAITING, *and*
SIR THOMAS LUCY.]

THE MINSTRELS

[*Singing.*]

Who would not sing on May-day,
On May-day,
On May-day,
Who would not sing on May-day
When Springtime is awake!
The mary-buds are paying
Bright gold for their delaying,
And fairy folk are straying
From out the wooded brake.

Who would not dance on May-day,
On May-day,
On May-day,
Who would not dance on May-day

And ring around the pole!
The hawthorn bush is pinking,
The lady-smocks are prinking,
And all this bobolinking
Makes quiring in my soul.

THE QUEEN

[Sinking upon the knoll.]

Cease your noise, madcaps.   You will set me to dancing ere I know it.

FILCH

Come, lads and lasses!   Swell your girths, and give a cheer for our good Queen Bess.

[They cheer stoutly.]

THE QUEEN

My thanks, loyal subjects.   The ship of state need never be becalmed, if the bellows of England blow so gustily.

LADY-IN-WAITING

This seems a brave adventure.

THE QUEEN

'Tis at least a time-whiler.

[FILCH *puts a cap over his doubled fist, which he has dotted with two black spots for eyes and, making his fingers move as if they were a mouth, speaks in a falsetto.*]

FILCH

Come buy of Filch,
Come buy of Filch,
Come buy of Filch, the Pedlar.
He'll sell you aught from brats to brains;
He'll laugh at you for all your pains;
He'll drain your cup
And snap you up
And prove a merry meddler.

THE QUEEN

I wager yon fellow is as full of quips and quillets
as the sea of brine. Ho, Pedlar! [FILCH *approaches
and bows*.] For how long has peddling been your profession?

FILCH

Beshrew my heart, Majesty, if peddling be my profession; 'tis but my recreation.

THE QUEEN

Indeed, merry lob! What call you your profession?

FILCH

An it please you, I am a skilled arithmetician;
quick at subtraction [*removing a ribbon from a nearby
lass*], able in addition [*adding the ribbon to his sack*],
keen at multiplication [*taking a purse with one hand
and a fan from the* LADY-IN-WAITING *with the other*],
and celebrated in division. [*Aside.*] Long division
for Filch and short division for t'others.

THE QUEEN

Arithmetics is a cold business—as hard as iron.

FILCH

Or steel!

THE QUEEN

You should find a softer one.

FILCH

Already have I done so.

THE QUEEN

How, fellow?

FILCH

I am an artist. I draw from life.

[*Removes a handkerchief from* SIR THOMAS'S *sleeve.*]

THE QUEEN

Mayhap if your artist skill match your wit I shall give you a pose.

FILCH

Marry, a pose from the Queen would be a poser for Filch. Nay, a pose from you is a posy for me; rather, a whole nosegay—not that your nose is gay; it puts me in mind o' a lily, 'tis so proud and pale.

THE QUEEN

Heigh ho, boiled brain! Your nonsense threats my poise, but the pose is yours.

FILCH

God mend me! My pose is but your poise blinded.

THE QUEEN

Unriddle your speech.

FILCH

What is pose but poise with its eye out?

THE QUEEN

Knave, you shall not have my pose in spectacles.

FILCH

Your beauteous pose shall be of itself the spectacle.

THE QUEEN

Fie upon you! [*Sound of bugles.*] The dancers!

FILCH

The dancers! Stand back, you gapes, if you would not get your toes cracked.

[*The bugles draw nearer. Enter* FRIAR TUCK *with solemn mien, bearing a heavy staff. The crowd cheers. He gravely makes the circuit of the clearing and drops his staff upon some obtruding toes. The victim shrieks.*]

FRIAR TUCK

Think not of self. Count thy beads and repent thee of thy folly. [*The crowd cheers and laughs. The* FRIAR *drops his staff on* SIR THOMAS'S *feet, which causes him*

to leap in pained surprise.]   Back! turn thee back while
yet there be time.   Thy feet, dancing as on a gridiron,
have strayed from out the straight and narrow path.
Say a pater-noster and 'ware thee o' purgatory.

[*The crowd roars.*]

THE QUEEN

Already you have a touch of purgatorial fires in
your toes, eh, Lucy?

[FRIAR TUCK *stands aside and the bugles again sound. Enter*
ROBIN HOOD *and the other morris-dancers, the* HOBBY
HORSE *and the* DRAGON *bringing up the rear. They dance.*
At the conclusion of the dance there is cheering, and the QUEEN
sends a purse to ROBIN HOOD.
Exeunt dancers to the sound of bugle, pipe, and bell. The crowd
follows with the exception of the QUEEN, WILL, BETSY, *the*
INDIAN BOY, SIR THOMAS, *the* LADY-IN-WAITING, FILCH,
and the MINSTRELS.   WILL *and* BETSY *await an oppor-*
tunity to approach the QUEEN.   FILCH *retires up stage to*
count his money and look over his wares.]

THE QUEEN

I have been vastly diverted.   [*To* SIR THOMAS.]
Sir Long Face, why do you not seek to amuse me?

SIR THOMAS

I, your Majesty?

THE QUEEN

Yea, you, my majesty!   Your visage hath been
washed in vinegar.

SIR THOMAS

You misjudge me.   I can be as rompish as a babe.
[*Looks around.*]   Ho, Pedlar!

FILCH

O Sir, most worthy Sir, here am I, Sir!

SIR THOMAS

Give me your drollest mask.

FILCH

[*Rummaging in his sack and bringing forth an ass's head.*]

This it is, your worthiness.   [*Aside.*]   'Tis his twin
brother.

[SIR THOMAS *claps on the head, tossing* FILCH *a coin which he
catches, bites, spits upon, rubs, and thrusts into his money
bag.* SIR THOMAS *makes his courtliest bow to the* QUEEN.]

SIR THOMAS

Speak, I bray you; I have ears for your slightest
word.

THE QUEEN

You graven image!   Now are you in truth in royal
favor.   Verily, two heads are better than one, though
one is—Sir Thomas's!

[WILL *and* BETSY, *with the baby, come forward.*]

WILL

An it please you, gracious Queen,—

LADY-IN-WAITING

Stand you back, chuff. Would you address her Majesty without permission?

THE QUEEN

I am inclined to yeaward. Bid them approach. Why, Sir Thomas! May I take eggs for money if this lad be not your youthful poacher.

WILL

But I did not poach, your Majesty.

THE QUEEN

What matters it, so long as you were forgiven?

WILL

It matters much to me.

THE QUEEN

Marry, the March-chick hath an ostrich conscience. How you did manage to hatch that giant bird out of your tiny shell, I wot not. Beware lest it swallow you whole.

WILL

Laugh, an you will, at my expense. I can afford to pay.

THE QUEEN

Would that you were my treasurer. Now, chick, what wish you of your Queen?

WILL

May it please your Majesty to help us restore this babe to his foster-mother.

[BETSY, *with a curtsy, holds forth the baby.*]

THE QUEEN

His foster-mother?   Who is she?

WILL

A Queen.

THE QUEEN

A Queen, say ye?

WILL

A most beauteous Queen.

THE QUEEN

[*Her glance cooling.*]

Indeed!   She must be fair.

WILL

'Tis said she hath the radiancy o' dawn and the grace o' twilight.

THE QUEEN

Who is your paragon,—Venus?

WILL

She is called Titania and is Queen of all the Fairies.

THE QUEEN

We know naught of your Titania. [*To* SIR THOMAS.]
What think you, Lucy,—this lad hath stolen from your
park; why not from the cradle?

SIR THOMAS

'Tis most likely, I should say.

THE QUEEN

Ass, look not so serious. [*To her* LADY-IN-WAIT-
ING.] Doth it not seem probable the boy hath stolen
the babe?

LADY-IN-WAITING

Certes, I vow you are right. Both the wench and
lad have a guilty look. And yet, they are seeking to
restore the babe, said they not?

THE QUEEN

Ay—they're doubtless tired o' their burden and
now would rid themselves of it. Ho, Pedlar!—eke
artist—eke arithmetician.

FILCH

Thrice at your service; and I come speedily, for my
peddling feet hope to run down a sale, my artistical
feet draw me with ease, and my arithmetical feet
bear me quickest of all because o' their numbers.

THE QUEEN

Then bid your three-fold feet bear you featlier than
ever. I would have them fetch a constable.

FILCH

Feet, do hear your Queen and Master? Majesty, they say every toe has a quadruple joint and that in each heel have the wings of Mercury feathered.

THE QUEEN

Away, Chatterbox! Your tongue has more joints than all your toes together. [*Exit* FILCH *on a run.* WILL *and* BETSY *move away.*] Stop, boy. A constable will take you and your babe in charge until your beauteous Titania has been found.

[SIR THOMAS *vainly endeavors to remove his mask-head.*]

SIR THOMAS

Will someone give me aid? I tire o' this folly.

[*The* MINSTRELS *go to his assistance, but the head will not come off.* WILL *and* BETSY *have moved near* SIR THOMAS. *Enter* FILCH *and the* CONSTABLE.]

FILCH

Here comes the law's staunch pillar, Majesty.

[*The* CONSTABLE *bows and scrapes, and scrapes and bows, pulling his forelock industriously.*]

THE QUEEN

Do not uproot your forelock, Master Constable, else what would be left with which to salute your Queen?

[*The* CONSTABLE *is stupefied with confusion.*]

FILCH

[*To* Constable *in whisper.*]

You still could scratch your head.

CONSTABLE

[*Brightening, and re-commencing his bows and scrapes.*]

Ah-yea, Queen, I cud scrattle m' yed.

THE QUEEN

Stand on your yed, mon, an it please you—but, marry, come up! what means this tangle?

[Sir Thomas *has been trying with mounting energy to remove the mask, and the* Minstrels *are tugging with might and main.*]

SIR THOMAS

Help! Deuce take the thing!

THE QUEEN

Lucy, I am your debtor. Never saw I more pleasing sight for laughter.

SIR THOMAS

Get me out o' this.

THE QUEEN

May I be carbonadoed if 'tis not a waggish spectacle. Will 't not come off?

[Filch *takes the baby from the arms of* Betsy, *who is absorbed in the struggle, and drops him into the sack.*]

ONE OF THE MINSTRELS

'Tis held by a thousand furies.

ANOTHER MINSTREL

'Twill not budge.

SIR THOMAS

I am dying of shame. Let me escape the sight of men.

[*He runs off*.]

THE QUEEN

Pshaw! the diverting play is over.

FILCH

It speaks well for the lasting quality o' my wares.

THE QUEEN

Hither, fellow! You went on our mission so featly we would give you our purse for your pains and entertainment.

FILCH

Not your purse, Majesty, O most sweet, sweet Majesty. I cannot take your purse.

THE QUEEN

Then name your own reward.

FILCH

I will take but one golden crown. And I will not

spend it. I will keep it to bear you in mind. One golden crown.

THE QUEEN

Take it, fellow, and welcome.

FILCH

[*Pointing forwards. All looking expectantly.*]

See yonder!

[*He removes the crown from the* QUEEN'S *head and drops it into his sack.*]

THE QUEEN

What mean you?

FILCH

Your pardon, Majesty, most, most sweet Majesty, but mine eyes, I fear, did play me tricks. Methought a sparrow was robbing a hawk's nest.

THE QUEEN

Let us to business. Master Constable, take into custody this babe and the lad and lass who stole it.

BETSY

[*Running forward, her arms outstretched.*]

Gone! the babe is gone!

WILL

The bronze nestling out of its cage! But it could not fly far.

[FILCH *slips off, right.*]

THE QUEEN

Impossible! Does neither of you know what has happed to the poor babe? Have you not hidden him?

WILL

Have search made, if you think it likely—in the crotch of yon tree—in a last year's acorn cup—in a mary-bud's pocket o' gold. There are a score o' places in which babes may be tucked away—out of sight o' the blind.

THE QUEEN

You prate saucily. Constable, let these children see the lining of the Town Cage till they confess their misdeeds. [*The* CONSTABLE *scratches his head.*] Ay, scrattle your yed, mon. All your wits are on the outside of it.

[*Raises hands to her head. Gives a cry and leaps to her feet.*]

LADY-IN-WAITING

Sweet Queen, what ails you?

THE QUEEN

My crown!

ALL

Your crown!

THE QUEEN

Gone!

LADY-IN-WAITING

Who could have taken it?

CONSTABLE

The gentleman Ass.

THE QUEEN

Body o' me, nay.   Sir Thomas hath not the imagination.

WILL

[*Banging his fist smartly on his hand.*]

The Pedlar!   Filch!

THE QUEEN

Boy, you have said.   He hath the wit and methinks he hath the roguery.

WILL

He went southward but a moment since.

THE QUEEN

Enough.   My crown!

WILL and BETSY

The babe!

[*The* MINSTRELS, *followed by* WILL, BETSY, *the* CONSTABLE, *the* LADY-IN-WAITING *and the* QUEEN *rush off stage shouting variously,* "*The crown!*" "*The babe!*"]

ACT III

SCENE: *The Forest of Arden in the moonlight.*
SIR THOMAS *is in the center of the clearing making fantastic and despairing efforts to remove the ass-head.*
Fairy bells tinkle. Enter TITANIA *and her train. Seeing* SIR THOMAS *they burst into peals of mirth.*

FAIRIES

Ring a ring a rosie,
What a funny nosey!
Here's a merry mortal
On our forest portal.
He's so big and eary
He shall be our deary.
Perfect time he keepeth
As his body leapeth.
How his feet are prancing,
Tuned to joyous dancing!
Bear him, gentle grasses—
He's the King of Asses.

[*They circle round him in a dance.*]

TITANIA

Oh, you roguish fellow! I do love you for your drolleries.

[*She sways in a gust of laughter.*]

SIR THOMAS

You mock me cruelly.   I would lose this head.

CADENCE

He wishes to lose his head.

CHALICE

Verily, he is the merriest ass mine eyes have looked upon.

SIR THOMAS

Give me air! give me air!

DULCET

If 'tis an heir you are seeking, pray take me.   I am as poor as a cathedral mousie.

MELODY

Ah, Dulcet, think you twice.   What if you should inherit those generous ears?

DULCET

I could drink in sweet sounds by the hogshead.

CADENCE

Or that prodigal nosey?

DULCET

I could follow it and never get lost.

SIR THOMAS

Give me air! give me air!

TITANIA

'Tis not an heir he wishes—'tis atmosphere in motion.

[*They wave their tiny fans about him in playful solicitude.*]

SIR THOMAS

Cease your fooleries! Have you no hearts?

TITANIA

[*Importantly.*]

Yea, I am growing one,—a veritable mother-heart.

[*The* FAIRIES *hang their heads.*]

SIR THOMAS

Then by that heart, I conjure you to hear me. I am full of misery because this ass-head hath been clapped upon my shoulders and clings thereto like a million leeches.

TITANIA

O thou poor dear! Come thou here and be comforted. Cadence! Dulcet! Chalice! Melody! Stand you back. You have no hearts and cannot know how this afflicted gentleman doth suffer. [*The* FAIRIES *sulk in the background.* TITANIA *leads* SIR THOMAS *to the knoll and seating him, caresses his head tenderly.*] Thou poor Ass! Titania's heart waxeth fuller and stronger with each glance at thee. [SIR THOMAS *gives a huge sigh.*] Here! put thy head upon my shoulder. Now art thou a peaceful Ass.

[*Tinkle of bells. Enter* OBERON, ROBIN, *and the* PUCKS. *At the sight of* TITANIA *and* SIR THOMAS, OBERON *pauses, dumb with rage, hand on sword-hilt.*]

SIR THOMAS

Is not my head heavy for your delicate shoulders?

TITANIA

Nay, most gentle and sympathetic Ass, not heavy—
but thy poor ears are over-large and hairy. [*She gives
her head a slight shake and blows a trifle of air through
her lips. Another sigh escapes* SIR THOMAS.] Yet are
they shapely ears, monstrous shapely ears, and soft, oh
soft, as the Humble Bee's waistcoat.

OBERON

Leave that odious monster!

[TITANIA *leaps to her feet.*]

TITANIA

Oberon!

ROBIN

[*Hopping about gleefully.*]

A brawl! a brawl! I do love a brawl!

TITANIA

[*To* ROBIN.]
You bedlam! [ROBIN *and the* PUCKS *laugh and play
leap-frog.*] Come, Fairies, our feet shall not tread the
same grasses as Oberon.

OBERON

Titania,—

TITANIA

Come, Fairies, come.

[*Exeunt* TITANIA *and the* FAIRIES.]

OBERON

[*Pointing to* SIR THOMAS.]

See the silly monster!

ROBIN

'Tis a dignified, solemn Ass.   Mayhap he will smile for us.

[*Tickles him with a twig.*]

SIR THOMAS

Cease your torments.

OBERON

How chances it you are in the soft graces of our Queen?

SIR THOMAS

She but strove to comfort me.

OBERON

You know otherwise, you doleful donkey.

ROBIN

Methinks he is a lying Ass.

PUCKS

A lying Ass!

SIR THOMAS

Mock me no further.   Take this effigy from my shoulders and by my goodly acres I will serve you to the top of your bent. I did but put it on to make sport for Queen Bess, and dearly have I rued it.

OBERON

Think you he speaks true?

ROBIN

He hath the earmarks o' something upon him.

COWSLIP

An they be the earmarks o' truth, then doth he speak a large, buxom truth.

ROBIN

He seemeth more goose than ass.

SIR THOMAS

But take off this hairy helmet and you may call me what you will.

OBERON

I have a fancy to believe you. You are so vile to look upon, our Queen could not have been moved by aught but disgust or pity. Are you ready to hearken to terms?

SIR THOMAS

Yea, right ready.

OBERON

A little Indian boy with a skin like bronze has been stolen.

ROBIN

By a lad and lass named Will and Betsy.

SIR THOMAS

I know the lad. He has poached at Charlecote.

OBERON

I am fain to have the babe. Keep wide open your eyes and patrol a part of the Forest this night. If you espy him, seize him. Should you find the wench and colt, take them prisoner and hold them till I come.

SIR THOMAS

It shall be done, my word on 't.

OBERON

Then, by the moontide flowing down,
Rid thy noddle of its crown.

[OBERON *touches the mask with his sword and* SIR THOMAS *lifts it off. He gives his head a huge shake and takes a deep breath of fresh air.*]

SIR THOMAS

I lose my head that I may find it.

OBERON

Fare you well. Remember!

[*They salute with their swords, then sheathe them.*
Exeunt OBERON *and* PUCKS, *left.* SIR THOMAS *takes another deep breath, feels his neck with pleasure, and drawing his sword, goes off, right.*

Enter FILCH, *rear. He looks about him, puts his tray near the knoll and dropping beside it takes the* INDIAN BOY *from his sack and cossets him.*]

FILCH

There, little recklin, no bigger than a fairy's minute, now shall we have a cuddle-time together. Whilst so wee, in my sack must you ride, as brave and snug as the Lord Mayor o' London Town. When you get higher and shed your pinny for strides, you shall jog along at my side and wheedle trade for us. I'll prank you up in all the bravery o' the shops and you'll never have call to blush for the two on us. [*The baby cries.*] Hush, you anointed bad one! Dry you up and you shall be fed full o' stuffed chine o' pork, with now and then a dash of roasted crabs. [*Louder cries.*] Hushaby, *hush!* I may have to warm your sallow skin wi' the flat o' my hand if you still not your squawks. [*More cries.*] I have it! You need to cut your wee bit teeth. Here's the very trick. [*Takes from his sack the* QUEEN'S *crown.*) There, lusty limb! Cut your teeth on that. Never was crown put to fairer use. [*The cries cease.*] I be a dabster! I take to nursing as a duckling to the pond. Now, my collop, I must forage for a bite to eat. First will I fetch a bowl of clear water that good fairies may find you and witches may not come anigh you. [*He lays the baby in the shelter of the knoll, the crown with him.*] Hold fast to your bauble. At last do I know what crowns be for—toys for babes to teethe on. [*He takes a small bowl from his tray and goes out, right. Returns and places the bowl beside the baby*.] There is the charm to keep you safe. What, little chuck, asleep so soon! [*Resumes his tray and looks upon the baby tenderly.*] Sleep you soft till you have rounded out your little dreams.

[*Exit* FILCH, *rear. A flash of red smoke, right, and the* WITCH OF WIMBLE *enters.*]

WITCH

This busy finger hath itched to do its work. [*Stirs with it.*] 'Tis time I had the brat again.

[*Goes to baby. Seeing the bowl she draws back in affright.*]

> Water for witch
> Cometh from ditch.
> Water that's pure
> Witch can't endure.

[*With her body drawn away she peers at the bowl.*]

Ha! a foul spot. A spinner hath fallen from a twig and smirched it.

[*Stoops to take the baby as* WILL *and* BETSY *enter. She stays motionless when she hears their voices.*]

BETSY

This is where Mother Hatfield of Pepper Alley said we would find the babe.

WILL

It is well we consulted her wisdom, for the White Witch finds lost things as the magnet lifts the needle to its bosom. [*The* WITCH *stoops swiftly for the baby, but before she can reach him,* WILL *runs forward and speaks in a ringing tone.*] Z! Y! X! W! V! U! T!

S! R! Q! P! O! N! M! L! K! J! I! H! G! F! E! D! C!
B! A! [*The* WITCH *cowers and shudders and backs off
stage, left.*] 'Tis a potent charm for routing witches.
I vow I say the criss-cross-row better tail up than
head up.

BETSY

My lamb! My cade lamb! My fleecy youngling!

[*Enter* SIR THOMAS.]

SIR THOMAS

Oho, hedgehog! tracked at last.

WILL

You are a keen hound to run the hedgehog to cover.
'Tis hard to tell whether you make better hound or ass.

SIR THOMAS

You prate without period or comma, boy,—you are
wordy as an almanac.

WILL

You have not the wit to read me.

SIR THOMAS

I've wit in plenty to have you flogged black and blue.

WILL

Black and blue? I like better my own color scheme,
for I'll pink you. [*Touches him with his sword.*] I'll
pink you till you're red.

SIR THOMAS

Give me the babe.

WILL

Marry, not a jot.

SIR THOMAS

Then will I cut my way to him.

[*Draws his sword.*]

WILL

You'll cut it through steel, an you do.

SIR THOMAS

Tush! Your weakling blade is a small bite for mine
to swallow.

WILL

It hath sharp teeth of its own and a stout stomach.
Have a care. [*They cross blades in a spirited contest.*]
Speed you up, Slowbones, else will I have lost and
found you again.

[*They continue fighting.*]

SIR THOMAS

Dolt!— — — — Urchin!

WILL

Pikeshead!

[WILL *has pressed* SIR THOMAS *to the edge of the clearing, and now
sends his sword spinning from his hand, playing his own
blade about* SIR THOMAS.]

SIR THOMAS

Beware, lad.   You might nip me.

WILL

Ay, that I might.   Mayhap already have I wounded your feelings.

SIR THOMAS

That was monstrous nigh my ear.

WILL

Listen to what it would tell you.

SIR THOMAS

That time it brushed against my nose.

WILL

Sneeze it away.

SIR THOMAS

Let me go, lad.

WILL

Am I poacher?

SIR THOMAS

You poacher?   Nay!

WILL

Dost swear it?

SIR THOMAS

Ay, lad.

WILL

Dost swear it by the three luces on thy family crest?

SIR THOMAS

May my luces turn louses if you be poacher. My keeper shall be dismissed for nabbing you. 'Twas a grievous error.

WILL

Nay, keep your keeper, and if you would keep whole your own skin, get you gone! [*Exit* SIR THOMAS *at a lively pace.*] Forsooth, he's a good runner.

BETSY

Oh, Will, you are a wondrous fine fighter. My heart so plumped against my ribs as I looked on you, I was fearful lest it get out of its cage.

[*Voices are heard.*]

WILL

Hide with the babe.

[*They go behind a clump of bushes. Enter* QUEEN ELIZABETH, *her* LADY-IN-WAITING *and the* MINSTRELS.]

THE QUEEN

I tell you 'tis a bootless search till we find that rascal, Filch.

LADY-IN-WAITING

Methinks Tyburn Tree is lonesome for him.

THE QUEEN

Tyburn shall have him. Oh my head! my head! What is a Queen's head without its crown? [*Enter* FILCH.] There is the mountebank now.

FILCH

How may I serve you, Majesty, most sweet, sweet Majesty?

THE QUEEN

Scape-gallows! where is our royal crown?

FILCH

Our crown, Majesty? Is it not on our head? Our hair is so golden 'tis brighter than the crown itself.

THE QUEEN

Give us the crown.

FILCH

D'ye mean, Majesty, there lives so vile a villain that he would poach on your beauteous preserves? And so excellently preserved, too!

THE QUEEN

Return the crown, and Justice shall be cheated of its rightful prey.

FILCH

I pray, justice or injustice, make me no prey. Filch is an honest fellow. May I eat fennel if I have the crown upon me.

[*Holds up his hands and turns around.*]

THE QUEEN

Nay, not upon you! You would see it were well hidden.

FILCH

[*Pointing to the crown, where it had rolled.*]

Here is *my* crown, Majesty.   Wear it till your own be found.

[*Extends it to her.*]

THE QUEEN

Your crown, wretch?   'Tis mine!   [*Seizes it and places it upon her head.*]   Now, Elizabeth's herself again.

FILCH

'Tis a most unholy wrong, Majesty.   I but shortly refused your purse, asking for no more than one golden crown.   May the artist in me be naught but thief an you did not say, "Take it, fellow, and welcome."

THE QUEEN

You mean—Oh, rogue, you'll be the death o' me! So much of sauce have you added to my day, beshrew me if I do not reward your diverting villainies.   Accept our purse.

FILCH

[*Weighing it in his hands.*]

Another purse!   A fat purse!   A purse with a paunch! I fear me I shall grow purse-proud in time.   When it comes to women, Filch likes 'em thin—[*bows to* QUEEN] ay, thin almost to angles, for what are angles but angels with their l's mixed—but when it comes to purses Filch'll angle for those himself, and the fatter the better.

THE QUEEN

A dance in the moonlight to still my pulsing feet!
Then will Elizabeth forsake the sweets o' the forest
for the sours o' the town.

[*The* QUEEN, *her* LADY-IN-WAITING *and the four* MINSTRELS
dance a gavotte. FILCH *has removed his tray, placing it
beyond the knoll out of sight, and has thrown himself on the
ground. He watches them as he chews a twig. Exeunt the*
QUEEN *and the other dancers.* FILCH *looks about in frantic
haste. Bells tinkle. Enter* OBERON, ROBIN, *and the* PUCKS.]

OBERON

What seek you with such warmth, mortal?

FILCH

O, dear Master Fairy! I am in sore trouble. I
seek a babe.

OBERON

What manner of babe?

FILCH

A wee babe, a most enchanting babe, with skin as
bronzy as an apple's russet coat.

OBERON

Rascal, you stole him! 'Tis the one I seek.

FILCH

Nay, good Sir, you mistake. I am an honest—

OBERON

Rogue. An honest rogue is honest only when he fulfils his rogueries.

FILCH

Marry, rogue I may be, with itching palm and prigging finger, yet who but I can take crowns from queens' heads, babes from mothers' arms, shoes from the very feet?

OBERON

Your steps have led you within the fairy-ring. [*Takes off his plumed cap and sweeps the air with it.*] Dog of a pedlar, down upon all fours, and from every midnight to cock-crow, go thus till you have repented of your deeds.

> By the Circle's mystic trend,
> Down upon all fours descend.

[FILCH *drops to his hands and feet and barks.*]

You have a strong bark. See that it steer you into clearer waters. [ROBIN *consults with* OBERON, *the* PUCKS *gambol, and* FILCH, *drawing near to* OBERON, *takes the* FAIRY KING'S *cap in his teeth, and unobserved, trots up stage and waits.*] Ho, lads! Let us search to the eastward.

[*Exeunt* OBERON, ROBIN, *and the* PUCKS, *right.* WILL *and* BETSY, *with the baby, come out of hiding.*]

BETSY

Look you about for a morsel of food for this poor manling. I vow his very soul is agog with hunger.

WILL

I'll see what the Forest will yield. If milk but grew on bushes!

[*Exit* WILL, *left.*]

BETSY

[*Laying the baby near the knoll.*]
Rest you, lambkin, till Betsy make herself more pleasing to the eye. I am roughed and blown by my wanderings.

[*Sits on the knoll, her back to the baby, smoothing her hair and costume.*
FILCH *stealthily runs forward, seizes the baby between his teeth, and goes off, back.*]

You are a precious boy. I wish I could ever keep you near me. [*Turns around; rubs her eyes.*] Saints protect!—where are you? Lambkin! call to your Betsy. [*Looks on all sides.*] 'Tis magic! Has the Witch come again? Will, O Will! where are you?

[*Exit* BETSY, *left.*
Tinkle of bells. Enter OBERON, ROBIN, *and the* PUCKS, *right.*]

OBERON

There is virtue in this spot tonight. The soil doth draw my feet unerringly.

ROBIN

It makes me light o' the heels.

[*Stands on his head. Enter left,* TITANIA *and her train. She is weeping silently.*]

OBERON

What do I see—Titania in tears?

TITANIA

Ah, Oberon, my heart is heavy!

OBERON

Heart, say you?

TITANIA

I have grown a, heart and oh, 'tis a mother-heart. Verily, my mother-heart is breaking for a sight of its babe.

OBERON

By my troth, never till now did I know how fondly you have wished for the Indian boy.   I thought it but a whimsey to cross my desire.

TITANIA

Nay, I am heartsick.

FAIRIES

[*Shaking their heads.*]

She is heartsick.

TITANIA

And full of longing.

FAIRIES

Full of longing.

TITANIA

Help me, Oberon.

FAIRIES

Yea, help her, Oberon.

OBERON

By the pipe of Dawn and the call of Dusk, you shall have the babe.   Is it not so, lads?

ROBIN and PUCKS

Ay, ay, sir!

OBERON

We shall seek the babe.

ROBIN and PUCKS

And find him!

OBERON

My sweet Queen, he shall be your own, no one's but yours.

TITANIA

Nay, my good lord, he shall be both yours and mine.

[*A puff of smoke and the* WITCH *enters.*]

WITCH

A pretty picture! a touching picture!   The Witch of Wimble is warmed to her marrow by scenes of loving reunion.

OBERON

What would you of us, beldam?

WITCH

I thought you might like to know where to seek the bronze babe.

TITANIA

My heart misdoubts me.   Trust her not, Oberon.

ROBIN

A pippin to a farthing the old dame hath flap-dragoned the babe.

WITCH

Hush, jackanapes!

ROBIN and PUCKS

[*Circling round the* WITCH.]

Flap-dragoned the babe! flap-dragoned the babe!

OBERON

Cease your carousal.   Why say you the Witch hath done aught to the child?

ROBIN

She may not have gulped him down whole, but I'll wager my white leather jerkin she hath guilty knowledge of him.

WITCH

The goblin spins tales out o' his impish fancies.

OBERON

Why speak you thus, Robin?

ROBIN

She stole the babe from our Queen to give to me.
Now I vow she steals him for her own uses. Think
you she comes here for good?

TITANIA

Give me my babe!

[*The* PUCKS *and* FAIRIES *threateningly surround the* WITCH,
OBERON *drawing his sword.* FILCH *trots in, rear, unobserved, stops up stage and watches the scene.*]

WITCH

Let me go and I will tell you who has the babe.

OBERON

[*Lifting his sword.*]

Hark you, Fairies.

WITCH

I have not the babe but I know who has.

ALL

Who?

WITCH

A graceless, interfering dullard, called Will. [FILCH
silently shows amusement.] He and the wench, Betsy,
had him within the hour.

TITANIA

Trust her not; but a short while since she deceived

me.　The weather-vane within me points to foul weather.

OBERON

What assurance give you that you speak in good faith?

WITCH

> By the old, prophetical law,
> By the hell-hound's bloodless paw,
> Tell I true of all I saw.

OBERON

On your double oath then, speak.

WITCH

Within the hour the babe lay near yonder knoll.　I sought to recover him for you when the madcap, Will, drove me off.　The wench was with him.　'Tis all I know.

OBERON

It is enough.　We will have vengeance on them.

FAIRIES and PUCKS

Vengeance.

[*Enter* WILL *and* BETSY, *left.　There are cries of, "They come!" "The lad!" "The wench!" "*WILL!*" "*BETSY!*"*]

WILL

What means your greeting?　It hath the warmth of a simoon.

TITANIA

Where is my sweet babe?   Why took you my treasure?

WILL

We look for him right ardently ourselves.

BETSY

That we may restore him to you.

WITCH

A likely tale!

WILL

[*To* TITANIA.]

We have sought you with our hearts for compass and, now we find you, we have not the babe.

TITANIA

The weather-vane within me that did point to "Foul" for the Witch, doth point to "Fair" for these children.

WITCH

Believe them not.   I tell you I saw this lad with the babe, on this very spot.   Ask him if 'tis true.

OBERON

Is this true?

WILL

I had him—

WITCH

Then where is he now?

BETSY

He was stolen from yonder knoll where I had placed him.

WILL

I was in quest of food for him.

BETSY

And when I turned to take the babe, he was *gone*.

TITANIA

I believe in these children. The Witch is at fault.

OBERON

They had the babe, and now they know naught of him. The children are to blame.

TITANIA

Fairies, seize the Witch!

OBERON

Pucks, the children!

[*There is a rush for the accused.* FILCH *barks long and loud. All pause in amazement.*]

OBERON

[*Drawing his sword.*]

That rascal here again!

WILL

Pray spare him, good Oberon. Pity his low estate.

BETSY

He may give us aid. Poor fellow, perchance to
your native wit hath been added the dog-gift of running creatures to cover. Find the dear babe and if
you would do him a kindness bring him hither. He
is in sore need of a mother.

WILL

Methinks a hungry spirit peers through the case-
ment of his eyes.

[*Exit* FILCH, *right.*]

OBERON

Spiders shall weave thick cords with which to bind
this lad and lass till truth has been plumbed to its
sullen deeps.

TITANIA

The Witch shall be surrounded by a horde of circling
bats. Round and round her shall they swirl and hold
her captive where she stands.

WITCH

Think you I fear your legion of flitter-mice? I'll
nip your charms with my magic.
Hoot! hoot! thou owl of night.

[*She listens, but the winds do not rush at her bidding.*]

Hoot! hoot! thou owl of night.

[*She listens again. Stamps in a passion of anger.*]

What hath drowned your voice, ye forces of the air?

TITANIA

Thou art in the fairy-ring!
Nevermore for deed of ill
Shall the forces work thy will.

WITCH

Nine times three and three times nine—
Demons, come ye forth and whine.
Quench the moon and stars that shine.

[*She looks expectantly about, then backs away.*]

TITANIA

Yea, go; I will not hold you captive.   Your poison
hath been drained.

[*Exit* WITCH.
Enter FILCH *with the baby.   He lays him gently at* TITANIA'S *feet.*]

BETSY

The babe!

TITANIA

[*Embracing the baby.*]

How he doth fit within mine arms!   Now am I
right glad of a heart.   'Tis a pillow for his head.   I
would thank you, friend, for bringing me my happiness.

OBERON

[*Touching* FILCH *with his sword.*]

By the grace that filleth thee,
Stand thou upright as the tree.

[FILCH *stands.*]

TITANIA

For a tiny soul-space, hold you the babe.

[*She gives him to* FILCH.]

FILCH

First I took him for love o' the game.   Next, I took him for love o' the boy.   But 'tis a mother's arms you need, bronzy bird, though you have made a nest of Filch's heart.

[*He gives the baby to* TITANIA *and lifts his tray from behind the knoll, dexterously taking* OBERON'S *sword as he leaves.   He calls lustily.*]

Come buy of Filch,
Come buy of Filch,
Come buy of Filch, the Pedlar.

[*Exit* FILCH.]

OBERON

Our thanks, lad and lass, for your courage.   Lass, next May-day come you here at dawn, and if you drink the drop of dew in the first mary-bud you spy, the wish dearest your heart shall come true.

BETSY

[*Joyously.*]

I know what I shall wish!

TITANIA

And, lad, now that I have a heart I can read yours.

You shall dream and make others dream.   On your
own hearthstone shall you find your fate.

[WILL *and* BETSY *stand aside.* TITANIA *with her baby,* OBERON,
*and all the members of their band, slowly sway in the moon-
light, singing a lullaby.*]

FAIRIES

Flame of night, thou nightingale,
Flush with song the forest trail.
Busy spider, whir thy loom
To the lilt of cherry bloom.
      East and West,
      Chant thy best,
      Fill with joy
      This, our boy.

Moon, when thou to cradle shrink,
Bid the babe serenely sink
In thy silver deeps to dream
Thoughts as chaste as candle-gleam.
      Undefiled
      Is our child.
      Tarry near,
      Hold him dear.

Fairies, swaying to and fro,
Teach the babe our spells to know,
And with torch of daffodil
Drive away the midnight's chill.
      North and South,
      Kiss his mouth,
      Beam with joy
      On our boy.

CURTAIN

EPILOGUE

SCENE: *The Kitchen on New Year's morning.*
WILL *is fast asleep on the hearthstone. The fire and
candles have burned out.*
Enter MISTRESS SHAKESPEARE, *who pauses amazed at
the sight of her boy. She tries tenderly to rouse him.*

MISTRESS SHAKESPEARE

Wake you up, laddie. [WILL *stirs but does not
waken.*] Oh, Will, my precious dreamer, why did you
not get into your bed? Wake you up! Wake you up!

[He slowly rises.]

WILL

Where am I?

MISTRESS SHAKESPEARE

In your home—where else of an early New Year's
morning?

WILL

'Tis not New Year's—'tis May-time. I was in the
Forest. How came I here? I must be dreaming.

[Rubs his eyes.]

MISTRESS SHAKESPEARE

Dreaming, my dearest? You have been making
dreams, but now you wake.

WILL

[*Looking at his side.*]

My sword!

MISTRESS SHAKESPEARE

[*Smiling.*]

What of your sword, lad?

WILL

It is vanished!

MISTRESS SHAKESPEARE

I fear you'll have sore search finding it.

WILL

[*Running to the table.*]

It has changed back to a knife.

MISTRESS SHAKESPEARE

My poor head feels as hollow as a deaf-nut. May-hap I'm the one who dreams!

WILL

[*Looking within the churn.*]

How comes it to be empty?

MISTRESS SHAKESPEARE

I'll not fill it till time for the churning.

WILL

What did you with the butter?

MISTRESS SHAKESPEARE

Butter?

WILL

'Twill not be fit to use.   A babe was in it.

MISTRESS SHAKESPEARE

A babe in the butter?   Oh, Will!   Will!

WILL

[*Going to the pot and gazing within.*]

I thought the Wimble Witch might have left a hot coal like a devil's eye, burning in the bottom.

MISTRESS SHAKESPEARE

The Wimble Witch!—'twill not do.   You must wake up. [*Takes him to the window.*]   Look out and see Henley Street of a wintry morning.

WILL

[*Looking out and turning in bewilderment.*]

Did not the dumb pedlar come to life?   Did not Betsy turn shepherdess?   And Titania get the Indian boy?   And—oh, Mother! did I not fight a duel with Sir Thomas and drive him forth at a merry pace?

MISTRESS SHAKESPEARE

Nay, lad, nay!   'Twas but a dream.

WILL

I tell you, it was true.

MISTRESS SHAKESPEARE

Nay, lad.

[The face of the pedlar, again dumb and stolid, peers through the window for a few moments, then disappears.]

WILL

'Twas truer than this room—than Henley Street I just now looked upon. I see it, hear it, yea, believe it. They came here—Robin, the Witch, the little Titania, Filch,—How prove you 'twas a dream?

MISTRESS SHAKESPEARE

I cannot prove it, lad, yet neither can you to me give proof. The testimony of all the years shows that some things are and other things are not.

WILL

Then shall I ever bear in mind my dreams,
And one day tune men's vision to my key.
Ah, music in one's dream hath sorcery
To woo the spirit to its tallest reach.
And laughter—how it riots to the brim
And tumbles over in a rainbow spray!
Each tear becomes a rounded crystal world,
With pictured pathos in its curvéd sides.
In waking do our joyance and our tears
And fine-wove mesh of music, stir us thus?
Our very lives are fabric of our dreams.
Then who dare say which be the realm of truth—
Our dreaming or our waking?

MISTRESS SHAKESPEARE

I cannot keep in step with you, my boy, yet do I try to follow where you lead.

WILL

Titania said I'd find my fate at home,
Yea, here at home, upon our very hearth!

[MISTRESS SHAKESPEARE *goes to the fireplace.*]

I almost fear to look; if 'tis not there
Perchance 'tis true a dream be but a dream.
She said 'twould be at home—on mine own hearth!

[*Slowly turns.   He stoops and gives a cry.*]

Behold 'tis here! my fate!

MISTRESS SHAKESPEARE

What mean you, lad?

WILL

[*Holding out a feather.*]

A pheasant quill—the pen with which to write
The stories in men's eyes, the songs that sing
For very joy of singing, all the dreams
That lap me 'round with shining witchery.

MISTRESS SHAKESPEARE

Why, laddie, there are teardrops in your eyes!
Mayhap a spinner, glum and overworked, hath nipped
your guiltless finger. Let me see.

WILL

Ah, Mother,—'tis not pain that starts my tears—

CURTAIN

GLOSSARY

(W) = Warwickshire dialect.

A

Addlepate = one of dull wit.
Afore = before.
Ah-yea (W) = yes.
Alack; alackaday = an exclamation of regret or sorrow.
An = if.
Anigh (W) = near.
Anointed (W) = innocently mischievous.
Apple-john (W) = a kind of apple that keeps a long time but becomes withered.
Aught = anything.
Ay = yes.

B

Bantling = a young child; an inexperienced youth.
Baubles = trinkets; gewgaws.
Bedlam = Bethlehem Hospital, or Bedlam, became an asylum for the insane in 1547.
Bedlam = a madman.
Beldam = a hag; a witch.
Belike = probably.
Bent = inclination.
Bergamo = a town in the Venetian territory, capital of the old province, Bergamasco, whose inhabitants used to be ridiculed as clownish.

Beshrew me   ⎫
Beshrew my heart ⎬ = evil befall me! plague on me!

Biggen (W) = a cap; especially a child's cap.

Bittock (W) = morsel.

Bits and bobs (W) = odds and ends.

Boiled brain = a hot-headed fellow.

Bonnie = comely.

Bootless = unavailing; useless.

Brave = fine; a general term of admiration or praise.

Brawl = a noisy quarrel.

Brawling = clamorous.

Bumpkin = an awkward rustic.

By my troth = by my faith; by my truth.

C

Cade (W) = gentle; mild.

Call (W) = cause; reason.

Carbonadoed = hacked or slashed, as meat prepared for the gridiron.

Caunt (W) = can not.

Certes = certainly; of a truth.

Changeling = something substituted for another; commonly used in the sense of one child substituted for another.

Charlecote = home of Sir Thomas Lucy, about four miles east of Stratford.

Chatterpie (W) = chatterbox.

Chine of pork = the back and loin of pork, commonly stuffed and flavored with a few leaves of aromatic bay. Especially served at the yearly festival of "The Mothering."

> "The lad and lass on Mothering Day,
> Hie home to their Mother so dear;

'Tis a kiss for she and a kiss for they,
A chine of pork and a sprig of bay,
A song and dance—but never a tear."

Chuck = a familiar term of endearment.
Chuff = churl; boor.
Collop = part of one's flesh.
Colt = a frisky youngster.
Constant (W) = always.
Cossets = fondles; pets.
Couldna (W) = could not.
Criss-cross-row = the alphabet.   In horn-books, the primers of early days, the letters were arranged to form a Latin cross, A at the top, Z at the bottom.   This was succeeded by the line form, crosses being placed at the beginning of the line; in consequence the alphabet was often referred to as "Christ-cross-row," "Chriss-cross-row," or "Criss-cross-row."
Crown = an English coin of the value of five shillings. Originally it was of gold, and was first coined in the reign of Henry VIII.   Since the reign of Charles II. it has been minted in silver only.

D

Dab (W) = a small portion of anything.
Dabster (W) = an expert.
Dalliance = idle behavior; dilatoriness.
Deaf-nut (W) = a hollow nut; a nut without a kernel.
Didna (W) = did not.
Dilling = a darling; a pet, especially a child born to an aged father.
Doant (W) = don't.

Doctor's stuff (W) = medicine; a remedy or potion.

Dollop (W) = a large portion of anything.

Dolt = blockhead; dunce.

Donna (W) = do not.

Doublet = a close-fitting outer body-garment, usually with sleeves, and sometimes with short skirts and belted at the waist. It came into use toward the close of the fifteenth century and was worn by men until the middle of the seventeenth century.

Dunch-dumpling (W) = a pudding made of flour and water and eaten with salt.

Dullard = a stupid person; dolt.

Den = even; evening.

E

Eggs for money, (to take) = to be put off with something worthless.

Eke = likewise; also.

F

Fain = earnestly desire.

Fell = melancholy.

Fennel = an "inflammatory herb;" it is aromatic and called by the old writers, "hot in the third degree."

Fie = shame upon you.

Flap-dragon = to seize and swallow, as in the game of flap-dragon (a game in which raisins and other edibles are snatched by the players out of burning spirits and swallowed.)

Flitter-mice = an old name for bats.

Forest of Arden = a forest lying to the west and north of Stratford. Villages and farmsteads were in clearings, and the Forest included a vast acreage.

Forewearied (W) = exhausted.

Forsooth = in truth; certainly.

G

Gapes = persons staring with open mouths.

Gewgaws = gaudy trifles; baubles; trinkets.

Giddy-pate = a scatter-brain.

God buy ye = God be with you (now contracted to "good-bye").

Golden Lion = a tavern in Stratford.

Good den = good even; good evening.

Good e'en = good even; good evening.

Guffaws = shouts of boisterous laughter.

H

Hap = happen.

Happed = happened.

Hedgehog (W) = a term of reproach, commonly applied to boys.

Henchman = a male attendant.

Hipped = derived from "on the hip," a term used in wrestling.

I

I' faith = in faith.

Inchling (newly coined) = one who is very diminutive.

Isna (W) = is not.

J

Jason = leader of the Argonauts. He won the sacred golden fleece by slaying the sleepless dragon that guarded it.

Jog = a slow trot.
Jog = nudge.
Jerkin = a jacket, short coat, or upper doublet.
Joyance = joy.

K

Ken = know.

L

Lady-smocks = cuckoo-flowers.
Lated (W) = belated.
Leather-coats (W) = russet apples.
Lob = a lout; a country bumpkin.
Loggerheads (at loggerheads) = to be engaged in a dispute or quarrel.
Longful (W) = anxious.
Luces = pike. Sir Thomas Lucy's coat-of-arms bore three silver luces, or pike. In "Merry Wives" the dozen white luces on the coat-of-arms of Justice Shallow become in the mouth of Sir Hugh Evans, a Welchman, "a dozen white louses."
Lucy (Sir Thomas) = a Warwickshire squire, supposed to have prosecuted Shakespeare sternly when the latter was about twenty-one, for deer-raiding in his park.
Luddington = a hamlet about three miles south-west of Stratford.
Lusty limb = a robust, roguish youngster.

M

Madcaps = those who are rash or giddy.
Manikin = a little man; a pygmy.

March-chick = a precocious youth.
Marry = an exclamation of surprise.
Marry come up = hoity-toity.
Mary-bud = the bud of a marigold.
Maut (W) = might (imp. of may).
Mayhap = perhaps.
Mekin' (W) = making.
Merrybone = marrow bone.
Mesel' (W) = myself.
Mewling = the crying of an infant; squalling.
Mill-sixpence = English coin struck during a period of
    fifteen years from 1561 to 1575, in comparatively
    small numbers.
Monstrous = very; exceedingly.
Morris-dance = name given to dances on May-day,
    etc., in which various personages were represented.
    (See descriptive note, *post.*)
Mortal (W) = extremely; extensively used by the
    rustic to indicate the extreme in anything.
Mountebank = a charlatan; a boastful pretender.
Mun (W) = must.

N

Na (W) = not.
Na (W) = not, used as a suffix, as in hadna (had not).
Nabbing = catching, or seizing suddenly.
Noddle = contemptuous term for head.

O

O' = of.
On = of.
Ŏŏt (W) = would you?

P

Pater-noster = the Lord's prayer.

Perforce = necessarily.

Pickthanks (W) = a captious person; a faultfinder.

Pikelet (W) = cake; a small cake.

Pikeshead = Sir Thomas Lucy's coat-of-arms bore three silver luces, or pike; hence the epithet, pikeshead.

Pilfer = filch; steal.

Pinny (W) = pinafore; apron.

Pother = turmoil; uproar.

Prank = deck gaudily.

Prate = talk vainly and foolishly; boast idly.

Prigging = thieving.

Prithee = I pray thee.

Purse-proud = puffed up by the possession of riches.

Q

Quillets = clever or witty turns or conceits.

Quips = verbal niceties; subtle distinctions.

Quiring = choiring; singing.

R

Recklin (W) = a child; a small child.

Ring a ring a rosie = a very old round.

S

Sanctus = a street in the western part of Stratford.

Scape-gallows = one who has escaped hanging, though deserving it.

Scraily (W) = attenuated; thin.

Scrattle (W) = scratch.

Scrumps = a small, sweet variety of apple.

Set my ten commandments in his face = an old Warwickshire expression, meaning to scratch the face
of another with all one's fingers.

Shilling = a silver coin originally issued by Henry VII.
In 1560 it was one-sixtieth of a troy pound of
silver.

Shive o' summat (W) = slice of something.

Shoodna (W) = should not.

Simoon (also, simoom) = a hot, dry wind of the desert.

Sin' (W) = since.

Slacken-twist (W) = a dawdler.

Slop (W) = a coat, short coat.

Sly-boots = a roguish, cunning, sly person.

Smudge (W) = kiss.

Sourings (W) = winter apples.

Spot (W) = a morsel. A *spot* is a lesser portion than a
skurrock, and a *skurrock* smaller than a *bittock*,
in Warwickshire dialect.

Spanking = swift, dashing.

Spinner = spider.

Strides (W) = trousers.

Stagger-bob (W) = calf.

T

Threefold Diana = the goddess presided in three
capacities, as Cynthia or Luna in heaven, Diana
on earth, and Hecate in hell.

Tidbit = a dainty.

Tiddington Road = a road leading from Stratford,
south of the Avon to Charlecote.

Tittle = the minutest quantity; a jot; an iota.

Top-full = brimming.

Tot (W) = a mug (especially a small mug).

T'others = contraction of *the others*.

Town Cage = the Stratford prison.

Trunks (or trunk hose) = a kind of full breeches extending from the waist to the middle of the thigh, worn in the sixteenth and seventeenth centuries.

Tyburn = the site of the Middlesex gallows. The gallows was called Tyburn Tree. Tyburn was a place of execution as early as the end of the twelfth century, and so continued until 1783.

U

'Ud (W) = would.

Upshot = the final outcome or result.

Urchin (W) = a term of reproach for a boy.

W

Wag = a droll fellow who says witty or humorous things.

Waggish = droll.

War (W) = was.

Wassail (Old English, Waes-hal, meaning, be well) = a spiced drink, commonly used on occasions of festivity or hilarity. What was popularly known as wassailing was the custom of trimming with ribbons and sprigs of rosemary a bowl which was carried around the streets by young girls singing carols at Christmas and New Year's. This ancient custom still survives in various parts of England.

Wench = a girl; a young woman.

Whut (W) = what.

Wight = elf; hobgoblin.

Wot (third person, sing. of wit) = knows.
Wotna (W) = would not.

Y

Yea = yes.
Yed (W) = head.   (M'yed = my head.)
Yent (W) = is not.
Yond (W and all English dialects) = yonder.
Youngling = a youngster.

NOTES

Titania, Oberon and *Robin Goodfellow* were re-created in *A Midsummer Night's Dream.*

"Titania" (taken from Ovid, Metamorphoses iv., 346, or (*id.*) iii., 173, where the name is applied to Diana), evidences the belief current at the time that the fairies were identical with the classical nymphs, and that Diana was their queen. Titania's more popular title was *Queen Mab.* (*Vide* Collancz' Preface to the play in the Temple Edition; Herford's Preface in the Eversley Edition.)

"Oberon" may be traced to the dwarf of that name in the Charlemagne romance, *Huon of Bordeaux*, translated from the French by Lord Berners about 1534 to 1540.

"Robin Goodfellow" is an English name for the mischief loving "Puck;" the latter probably of Celtic origin, but found in English prior to the Conquest, and early in Scandinavian and other dialects. The German equivalent of "Robin Goodfellow" is "Knecht Ruprecht." (*Vide* Collancz, *supra*.)

The little Indian boy is the cause of dispute between Titania and Oberon in the Shakespeare play.

PROLOGUE

Page 8. *My heart is built in the shape of a W:* During the reign of Elizabeth, out of compliment to the Queen, many houses, including Charlecote, were built in the shape of an E. The plan derives its name from three projecting entrances in the façade, each provided with a porch. These gave the ground plan the shape of an E, with stubby arms.

Page 9. *There's fell need for the perfumer:* In Elizabethan times rushes were strewn upon the floors. When it was necessary to re-rush a room, fresh ones were deposited upon the old. "And a room was not always purged of its rushes more than once a year. The result was filth, more or less absent to the eye, but present to the nose. The latter condition gave rise to a whole profession, as necessary and as distinctive as that of the chimney sweep; namely, the perfumer. It was his business to come, when a room had grown too foul to live in, in order to remove the stench by burning juniper wood and other sweet smelling herbs. Vermin flourished under such conditions, and many are the allusions that could be cited referring even to royal visits, from which persons returned bitten from head to foot." (From Henry Thew Stephenson's *The Elizabethan People*.)

Page 13. *I relished the sight of our Queen at Kenilworth last July*: At Kenilworth Castle, which is about fifteen miles from Stratford, the Earl of Leicester, in July of 1575, entertained Queen Elizabeth and devised pageantry and splendid ceremonies in her honor. Scott has recorded its brilliancies in his novel, *Kenilworth*.

Page 23. *Sir Thomas Hunt* is thought to have been Shakespeare's master at Grammar School from 1572 to 1577, and, if so, he doubtless contributed greatly to the development of the poet's mind. He was a man of erudition. His title was given him in accordance with the custom of the times to bestow titles upon schoolmasters of note.

Page 24. In 1575, *Richard, Anna, Joan* and *Gilbert Shakespeare* were one, four, six and nine years of age, respectively.

Page 25. *Witches and their tailless kind:* Tradition held that witches, though able at will to assume the form of any animal, had to dispense with the tail. The lack of it was frequently the cause of detection of witches in their disguised forms.

Act I

Page 41. *My bonnie beard:* The beard was a well known characteristic of witches.

Act II

Page 51. *May-day dew* was used as a beautifier of the complexion. The young people went a-Maying, rubbing their cheeks with early dew to secure fresh coloring for the ensuing year. Samuel Pepys, in his Diary, says:

"My wife away to Woolwich in order to a little ayre, and to lie there tonight, and so to gather May-dew tomorrow morning, which Mrs. Turner hath taught her is the only thing in the world to wash her face with."

Page 55. *May all my teeth be strung on lute strings*, etc.: Lutes were the favored instruments to accompany singing. Every barber shop had lutes and zitterns for the entertainment of those patrons who were obliged to wait. Barbers of those times were usually minor surgeons, their most important and frequent operation being the drawing of teeth. They tied the extracted teeth on lute strings and displayed them in front of their shops as signs. To this day, in a somewhat changed form, the custom survives in London.

THE MORRIS-DANCE

Page 61. The following description of the old morris-dance is paraphrased from that of Strutt, the antiquarian, found in his romance, *Queenhoo-Hall* (vol. I., p. 13, *et seq.*):

First enter *Friar Tuck* (as indicated in the text of this play), then enter:

Six young men, as woodmen, clothed in brown, axes upon their shoulders, and garlands of ivy leaves about their heads;

Six girls, as milk maidens, in blue kirtles, bearing shining pails;

Six foresters, in green, each carrying a bugle-horn which he sounds as he enters;

Robin Hood, in a bright green tunic, gold-fringed, with blue and white hose and hood, a bugle-horn, a sword and dagger, a bent bow in his hand, arrows at his girdle and a garland of rose-buds on his head;

Little John at Robin Hood's right hand;

Will Stukely at Robin Hood's left;

Ten other attendants of Robin Hood, who, together with Little John and Will Stukely, are clad in green, with bows in their hands and arrows in their girdles;

Two maidens in orange-colored kirtles with white courtpies (short vests), strewing flowers;

Maid Marian in a watchet-colored (light blue) tunic reaching to the ground, over which is a white rochet (a linen outer garment), loose-sleeved, with silver fringes, a cloth of silver girdle having a double bow at the left, her fair long hair flowing, topped by a net of gold upon which is a garland of silver and violets. She is supported by

Two brides-maidens in light blue rochets with crimson girdles, garlands of blue and white violets upon their heads;

Four maidens in white costumes, with green courtpies, and garlands of violets and cowslips;

The Fool bearing a pole with an inflated bladder on one end;

The May-pole borne by *eight youths;*

The Hobby-Horse and *The Dragon* bringing up the rear.

Attached to the wrists, elbows and ankles of the dancers are bells of varying sizes and tones.

With the appearance of the May-pole the foresters sound their horns and the spectators cheer while the pole is being elevated. The woodmen and the milk maidens dance around it in rustic fashion to the music of pipe and tabour. At the conclusion of the dance, the one who undertakes to play the Hobby-horse comes forward with his appropriate equipment, frisking back and forth, galloping, curvetting, ambling, trotting, to the delight of the spectators. He is followed by the Dragon, hissing, roaring and shaking his wings with astonishing ingenuity. To round out the mirth, the Fool capers here and there between the two monsters, now and then slyly casting handfuls of meal into the faces of the gaping rustics, or rapping them upon their heads with the bladder. The Hobby-horse at last begins to falter in his paces, and his rider orders the Dragon to fall back; the well-nurtured beast, being out of breath, readily obeys, which concludes this part of the pastime.

Concerning the Hobby-horse and the Dragon, Stephenson gives Drake as authority for saying that the Hobby-horse consists of the head and tail of a horse made of paste-board and attached to a person whose business it is. while seeming to ride gracefully on the back of the animal, to imitate its curvet-tings and prancings, the horse's supposed feet being concealed by a footcloth reaching to the ground. The Dragon, constructed of the same materials as the horse, is made to hiss and vibrate its wings, and is subject to frequent attacks by the man on the Hobby-horse, who then personates the character of St. George.

The dance above outlined is but one of many morris-dances. One of the simpler forms may be substituted for that described above, or the number of performers may be reduced as cir-cumstances require. One of the old morris-dance tunes should be used.

For an extended discussion of the morris-dance see *The Morris Book* by Cecil J. Sharp and Herbert C. MacIlwaine, Novello & Co., London, 1912, and the companion work by the same authors, entitled, *Morris Dance Tunes*.

The Drama League of America has issued a pamphlet on old folk dances, including morris-dances, with suggestions as to the music. This pamphlet may be secured for ten cents at the League's headquarters, Marquette Building, Chicago.

Act III

Page 79. *A bowl of clear water:* Well-wishing fairies were likely to be attracted by a clean room and a bowl of clear water.

Page 80. *The White Witch finds lost things:* A White Witch was a kind of novice, indulging in insignificant witcheries. These witches were regarded as harmless, often living among their neighbors in the friendliest relations. "They told for-tunes, exercised the arts and practices of palmistry and ele-mentary astrology, dealt out simples for a substantial con-sideration, cast waters and furnished love potions to distressed and disappointed youths and maidens. We learn from *The Wise Woman of Hogsden* a list of the notable White Witches then in fashion. . . . Mother Hatfield in Pepper Alley was useful in finding lost things, a task in the performance of which she was especially famous." (From *The Elizabethan People*.)

Page 81. *'Tis a potent charm for routing witches:* Witches

were exorcised by charms, frequently made of a senseless succession of syllables, or of sentences, said backward. The Lord's Prayer, recited thus, was considered peculiarly efficacious.

Page 88. *Your steps have led you within the fairy-ring:* A little circle in the grass of a brighter green, within which the fairy folk danced by night, was called a fairy-ring. It was held unsafe for one, other than a fairy, to venture within, else he would be subject to magic spell.

Page 98. *Nine times three and three times nine:* Multiples of three and nine were particularly affected by witches, both old and new. In Fairfaxe's "Tasso" (book xiii., stanza 6), we read:

"Witchcraft loveth numbers odd."

In Macbeth, one of the witches says:

"Thrice and once the hedge-pig whined,"

rather than make use of the even number, four.

Printed in the United States of America.

THE following pages contain advertisements of a few of the Macmillan books on kindred subjects.

The Steadfast Princess

By CORNELIA L. MEIGS

Cloth, 12mo, $.50

This play for children, selected from hundreds of manuscripts submitted in the contest, won the prize offered by the Drama League of America. The story is of a princess who remains true to her ideals despite the temptations of circumstances and the obstacles which seek to prevent her from fulfilling her duty to the people over whom she rules. In the end she is happily rewarded, as is natural for so steadfast a heroine. The play is of the sort which children enjoy giving as well as seeing.

THE MACMILLAN COMPANY
Publishers   64–66 Fifth Avenue   New York

TRUE STORIES OF GREAT AMERICANS
(New Volumes)

Ulysses S. Grant
By LOVELL COOMBS

Abraham Lincoln
By DANIEL E. WHEELER

Daniel Boone
By LUCILE GULLIVER

Lafayette
By MARTHA F. CROW

Each volume illustrated. Decorated cloth, 12mo, $.50

This series of biographies for young people, the first volumes of which were published in the spring of 1915, has now established itself as one of the most valuable literary projects of recent years in the juvenile book world. The volumes have all been well planned. The authors have, without exception, known how to secure, and hold the attention of the average boy and girl. They have written entertainingly, without sacrifice of facts. Each book gives a full length picture of the particular great man with whom it is concerned.

THE MACMILLAN COMPANY
Publishers   64–66 Fifth Avenue   New York

The Mastering of Mexico

By KATE STEPHENS

With maps and half-tone plates. Decorated cloth, 12mo.

This is a simple, close-knit story of adventure founded on eye-witness accounts of one of the sixteenth century conquerors. Verisimilitude is kept even to the use of the *I* form of narration. The conquest of Mexico was one of the most picturesque military exploits in all history. How the doughty Spaniards made it a community, democratic affair and how that fact insured its success, the three hundred and fifty pages of this book tell in limpid, idiomatic English.

———

THE MACMILLAN COMPANY

Publishers   64–66 Fifth Avenue   New York

The Life of William Shakespeare

By SIR SIDNEY LEE

With portraits and facsimiles. New edition rewritten and enlarged. Cloth, 8vo, $2.00

This standard biography of Shakespeare, originally published seventeen years ago, is now reissued in new form. It has been drastically revised and greatly enlarged. Recent Shakespearean research has proved unexpectedly fruitful. The author's endeavor has been to present in a just perspective all the trustworthy and relevant information about Shakespeare's life and work which has become available up to the present time. The text has been reset throughout and runs now to 758 large pages, a sufficient commentary on the extent of the labor which this edition represents.

THE MACMILLAN COMPANY

Publishers   64–66 Fifth Avenue   New York